2021 ENERGY ALMANAC

THE HUMAN CONNECTION TO THE SUN, MOON, STARS & PLANETS

Sherry Hopson

Wallis Suda

EDITED BY
SAMANTHA KEITH
JENNIFER EISENBRAUN

To

Wallis, my inspirational muse.

Marni, the leader of leaders.

Jackie, the door opener to an incredible journey.

I am grateful.

CONTENTS

THE UNIVERSE & YOU

Our universe's sun, moon, stars, and planets create energy in different forms of frequencies, gravitation, and electromagnetic waves. The ebbs and flows from the vast content of varying energy contribute to balance and harmony for all life on our planet. Everything within our universe reacts to energy. All have the purpose of supporting us, nurturing us, developing us, and triggering our instincts for the flow of nature.

The creation of our reality and our existence within our reality comes from our reaction to energy patterns. Human beings are made from energy, starting from the molecular composition of our physical body. Every emotion, every thought, creates frequencies within our cells. The energy within an environment can alter our cellular frequencies. If our environmental energy frequency is high, it can influence us to experience a healthier body. If it's lower, we experience a sicker body. A healthy body typically has a frequency ranging from 62 to 78 Hz, while many diseases begin to show up at 58 Hz.

Our bodies are made to shift and change with our emotions and environment through energy grids known as meridians. We have 15 meridians in the body that are connected together through meridian points. These energy grids allow the rivers of energy to flow to our different systems and organs. When we feel sick or blocked, it is most likely from the results of the meridian points being disconnected and blocking the energy flow. The body has hundreds of chakras, but only 12 chakras are considered the main influencers of energy, interacting with physical and metaphysical energies creating a balance between the two. These energy centers are attached to our meridians and act as conduits, sending and receiving energy to and from our environment. When our chakras receive energy, they interpret frequencies and vibrations, translates them into our emotional language, relays the information to our nervous system, creating our reactions. When we send energy from our body, our emotions are turned into vibrational waves in meridian points then to the chakras to be released to our environment. Like other animals, we are designed to sense danger or safety within our environment and from others. Walking into a room and sensing something is wrong, out of place, or unbalanced is our chakras at work.

The planets in our solar system carry different frequencies and vibrations. Some planets have reputations. In ancient history, the planets were associated with Gods and Goddesses portraying the personal traits of the planets' energy. Mars, for example, is the energy of war, and Venus is the energy of love. Energy waves containing these frequencies translate to emotions in our bodies when received through our chakras. Each frequency has a corresponding emotion to it. The lower the frequency, the more negative emotions we experience. The higher frequencies will create positive emotions. During the planets' orbital phases around the sun, we experience the frequencies' changes through the meridian girds on Earth. When the planet is indirect (or behind the sun, shielding the energy), the frequencies will become weaker. The shifting of emotional and physical energy occurs while planets enter into retrograde phases. Depending on other planets' position, moon phases and your own health will determine the levels of emotional shifting you feel during a retrograde.

The Earth's orbit around the Sun and the Moon around the Earth change the gravitational pull throughout our day. The gravitational pull affects us by changing the flow of fluids in our bodies and changes our chakras' shape. Our chakras' shape extends and is longer during full moons or super moons, creating a more prolonged energy wave intensifying our emotions. The water in our bodies also flows faster, creating a detoxing effect heightening emotional levels. This is why it feels like the crazies come out during full moons. During the other phases of the moon, like crescents, the gravitational pull lessens. The shape of the chakra changes and shortens, reducing the frequency waves and creating a more relaxed emotional response.

The connections we have to our universe are necessary to trigger our primitive instincts for our bodily changes, survival with the fight and flight responses, and the energy reactions needed to create our realities. When contributing negative emotional frequencies to the environment against the universe's natural flow, we create imbalances. Flowing against nature is like taking the long route to your destination on the road full of potholes and detours. We create hardships, blocks, and eventually, physical disease.

Our energies are incredibly fluid. They are meant to change from moment to moment. When we are out of balance, stuck, or blocked due to the influence of a planetary aspect, we can use any of our five physical senses to balance our emotions. Our senses can be used to evoke memories of pleasure, joy, and happiness to bring us back into alignment. Remedies like aromatherapy, sound waves, or acupressure, to name just a few, create change in our emotions. They negate the planetary influences by changing our frequencies. During certain phases, some frequencies benefit you, and there are opportunities to amplify your energy.

The 2021 Earth grids bring energies of change by expanding communications and completing projects. There is also the destruction of agreements or contracts that will bring about a rebirthing in 2022. A series of star alignment that occurred in 2019, opened up our chakra system for expansion. An expansion occurs when the electromagnetic frequencies change, and the body needs to create a new balance between the physical and spiritual self. The last chakra expansion humans experienced was in 1917, creating a connection in the heart chakra to change. This current expansion is creating a new chakra located on the back of the head, allowing more creative influences on the planet, also marks the beginning of the age of Aquarius. The expansion is creating an amplification of emotions in the body which is one of the factors bringing about the pandemic. The cycle is a five-year cycle, ending in 2024. During 2021 emotions will still be running high, adding to the destructive energy on the Earth plane. Extra care is needed to detach from the negative emotions by focusing on creating new projects or artistic endeavors. The year 2021 also brings higher than normal pregnancy rates from the end of March to the end of August. Good for those trying, or a surprise for those who aren't. There will also be unusual weather patterns between March and August. The energy of support for building new foundations in finance and career will start in July through the year's completion.

Throughout the book, I will share remedies and amplifiers for different energy aspects to enhance your emotions positively.

THE MOON

FULL, NEW, SUPER & ECLIPSES

THE MOON

The moon plays a significant role in contributing energy to our planet and influences our culture. In Roman mythology, Diana, the moon goddess, was known for the hunt and fertility. Ancient fishermen learned to fish according to the moon cycles to ensure a bountiful catch. Native Americans named each full moon to align with the cycles in nature.

Recent research shows that the moon cycles' affects changes in our bodies and our emotional well-being. The moon cycles through 8 phases over a 29.5-day period. Three cycles affect our energy more than the others, the new moon, the full moon, and the waning crescent. The gravitational pull from the moon and the sun that affects the ocean tides also creates a constant change in physical body fluids. This gravitational pull also creates emotional and physical changes throughout the cycles. If the sun and the moon are strong enough to move oceans, imagine the power it has over your body's 60% water composition.

FULL MOON

The full moon occurs when the sun, Earth, and moon are in alignment.

FULL MOON ALIGNMENT

The full moon amplifies our emotions resulting in a rise of pregnancies, crime, accidents, anxiety, and suicides. The increase of heightened emotions and reactions are due to the moon's gravitational pull changing our source and karmic chakras to become elongated in shape. This shape creates a prolonged energy wave within the chakras, amplifying our emotions, good or bad. When our emotions are negative, our chakra points will become unbalanced disconnecting a flow of energy to the meridians. The increase of negative emotions nudges us or sometimes pushes us to seek change in our life, resulting in learning and wisdom for our emotional growth.

The source chakras are 12 main energy centers for the body that link the physical and spiritual bodies together for balance. Karmic chakras are energy centers created from emotional and physical wounds. During the moon cycles when there is a pull on the chakras, if any of the chakras are weaker due to negative beliefs, thoughts or environmental patterns, the emotional aspect of the moon cycle will have a greater effect. The gravitational pull can last as long as three days during a typical full moon and as long as five during a super moon. The super moon occurs when the moon is the closest distance to the Earth in its orbit.

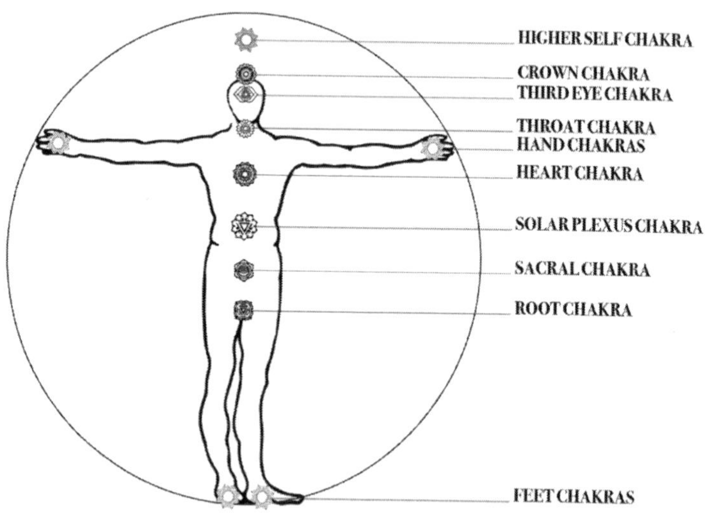

CHAKRA SYSTEM

FULL MOON RITUAL

Full moon rituals have dated back for thousands of years in many cultures, honoring the rhythms of life. Rituals are a series of actions performed according to a prescribed order and were usually designed to bring an individual something he lacked or ease his day-to-day life.

When the full moon elongates the chakras' shape, a prolonged energy wave occurs, amplifying the emotions. This occurrence offers us the opportunity of tapping into the spiritual, healing, and manifestation potential of its energy. Placing the mind and body into the correct state will open the chakras wider, creating a greater vibrational change. Each step is important and needs to be followed in order.

1. Write a gratitude list with at least 15 items: opens the heart chakra.

2. Drink a floral relaxing tea: Chamomile, Valerian Root, St John's Wort, for example, relaxes the nervous and digestive system allowing the mind to relax.

3. Repeat the word OM in a chant for 3 minutes, draw the word OM out for as long as you can each time you say it: opens the crown and third eye chakras.

4. Stand with your feet 2 feet apart and sway from right foot to left foot like you are rocking back and forth for 15 minutes. The rhythm of the

rocking balances all the chakras and opens them to the flow of energy.

5. Write an I am intention statement for your next month: your I am statement should be a strengthening or door opening statement, I am loved or respected or successful, for example.

6. Plant the I am statement in dirt and harvest on the next full moon: The planting of the statement creates a powerful connection of intention to the subconscious mind. Subconsciously the action of planting something has the meaning of growth for most people, and for some, you reap what you sow.

NEW MOON

The new moon occurs when the sun and the moon are aligned, with the sun and the Earth on opposite sides of the moon.

NEW MOON ALIGNMENT

The gravitational pull is weaker, our chakras shorten, lessening the energy wave, causing our emotional reactions to dissipate. The new moon represents a time to start new ventures, new relationships, new beginnings. The void of exaggerated emotions will create a smoother union. The energy exists during this cycle for 4.5 days.

WANING CRESCENT MOON

The waning crescent is the last phase before the new moon. The moon's left side illuminates a small crescent while the Earth's position blocks the rest of the moon.

WANING CRESCENT MOON

This moon phase is nature's rest period. We are not being pushed or pulled by the gravity of the sun or moon. It is best to complete, organize, and create during this period, getting us ready for the new moon and new beginnings. This period lasts for 5 days.

WANING CRESCENT MOON DATES

JANUARY	1 2 3 4 5 6 **7 8 9 10 11 12** 13 14 15 16 17 18 19 20 21 22 23 24 25 26 27 28 29 30 31
FEBRUARY	1 2 3 4 **5 6 7 8 9 10** 11 12 13 14 15 16 17 18 19 20 21 22 23 24 25 26 27 28
MARCH	1 2 3 4 5 6 **7 8 9 10 11 12** 13 14 15 16 17 18 19 20 21 22 23 24 25 26 27 28 29 30 31
APRIL	1 2 3 4 **5 6 7 8 9 10 11** 12 13 14 15 16 17 18 19 20 21 22 23 24 25 26 27 28 29 30
MAY	1 2 3 **4 5 6 7 8 9 10** 11 12 13 14 15 16 17 18 19 20 21 22 23 24 25 26 27 28 29 30 31
JUNE	1 2 **3 4 5 6 7 8 9** 10 11 12 13 14 15 16 17 18 19 20 21 22 23 24 25 26 27 28 29 30
JULY	1 **2 3 4 5 6 7 8 9** 10 11 12 13 14 15 16 17 18 19 20 21 22 23 24 25 26 27 28 29 30 31
AUGUST	**1 2 3 4 5 6 7** 8 9 10 11 12 13 14 15 16 17 18 19 20 21 22 23 24 25 26 27 28 29 30 **31**
SEPTEMBER	**1 2 3 4 5 6** 7 8 9 10 11 12 13 14 15 16 17 18 19 20 21 22 23 24 25 26 27 28 29 **30**
OCTOBER	**1 2 3 4 5** 6 7 8 9 10 11 12 13 14 15 16 17 18 19 20 21 22 23 24 25 26 27 28 **29 30 31**
NOVEMBER	**1 2 3** 4 5 6 7 8 9 10 11 12 13 14 15 16 17 18 19 20 21 22 23 24 25 26 27 **28 29 30**
DECEMBER	**1 2 3** 4 5 6 7 8 9 10 11 12 13 14 15 16 17 18 19 20 21 22 23 24 25 26 27 **28 29 30 31**

January

THE WOLF MOON

The emphasis of this month's moon energy cycle is on relationships. The focus of who we are in a relationship. The emotional aspects of need, balance and commitment will become stronger between the last day of the New Moon on the 15th until the day before the Full Moon on the 27th.

New Moon 13th

Unbalancing of the chakra: Sacral Chakra

Emotional results: Feeling irritated, not belonging, feeling lost, low creativity

Physical results: Sexual glands, reproductive organs, intestinal tract, colon, lumbar region, pelvis, hips, kidneys, circulatory system, bodily fluids (lymphatic)

Spiritual results: Feeling of disconnect

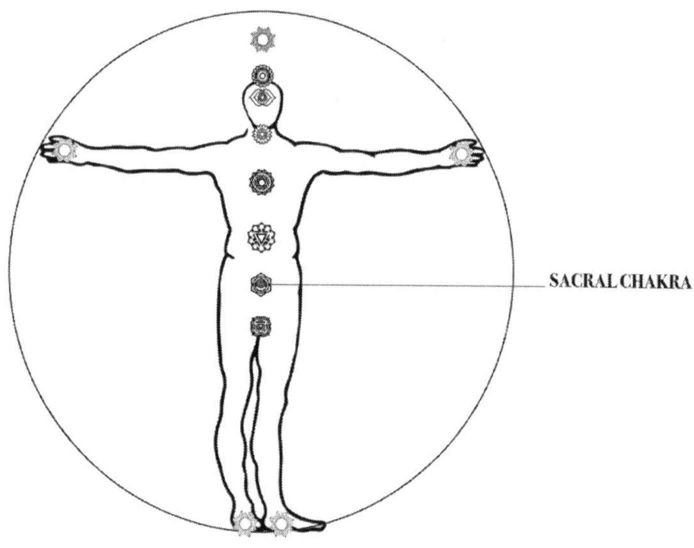

Remedies:

- Movement: Traveling to new geographical area
- Aromatherapy: Baths with essential oils of sandalwood, mint or lavenders
- Body: Higher levels of vitamin D supplement

- Sound therapy: Classical music Tchaikovsky or tuning fork 4096C
- Journal exercise: Writing all the reasons why you belong and are connected

Growth opportunity:

- Noticing your emotional triggers and not responding to them. Allowing yourself to understand the emotion to change the reaction.

Full Moon 28th

Remedies:

- Movement: Exercise early evening hours, massaging of acupressure points above the top of the right and left inner ankles
- Aromatherapy: Any essential oils in the evergreen family

Mantras

I am graduating from my past, leaving my old patterns behind to create new ones that bring fulfilling relationships that I need and desire.

Or

I am creating, receiving and experiencing a perfect harmony in my relationships.

February

THE SNOW MOON

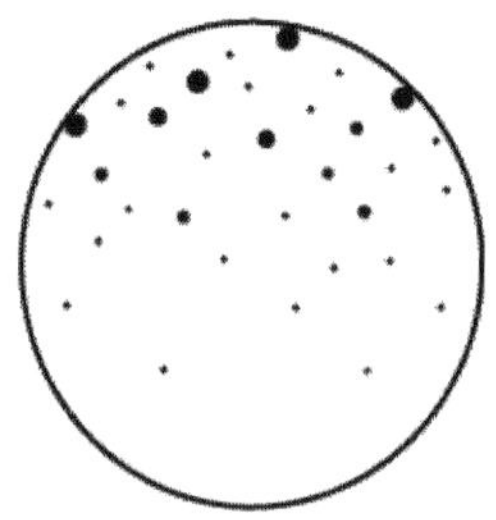

The emphasis of this months' moon energy cycle is our passions. The focus of exploration of our passions using our senses and opening pathways to our passions, will become stronger beginning February 14th until the day before the full moon February 26th.

New Moon 11th

Unbalancing of the chakras: Throat & Feet Chakras

Emotional results: Feeling of not being heard, voice not strong enough, indecisiveness, easily frustrated, irritated

Physical results: Throat, thyroid, lymph nodes, sinus infections, ear infections, weak ankles or swelling of the ankles

Spiritual results: Increase of daydreaming, trying to connect to path

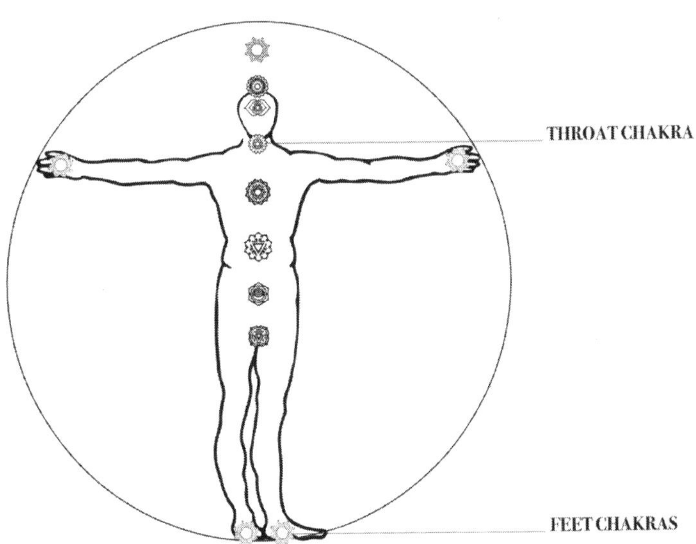

Remedies:

- Movement: Stretching and rolling the ankles
- Aromatherapy: Gardenia or basil essential oils

- Body: Calcium supplements
- Sound therapy: Mozart concertos
- Journal exercise: Trusting in your heart's desire, write down what you would like to experience and know that you may have it

Growth opportunities:

- Discovering new passions to explore in your life
- Explore your childhood memories of what you liked and desired, and follow your heart

Full Moon 27th

Remedies:

- Energy Cleansing: Sage and Palo Santo burning
- Body: Sage tea, apricot tea, sea salt cleansing bath

Mantras

My dreams are coming alive created by my passions, directing me and fulfilling me.

Or

I am living an elevated life, one of discovery, excitement and learning.

March

THE WORM MOON

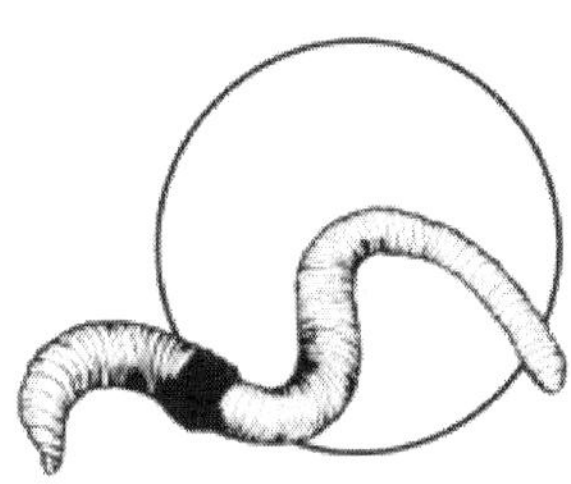

The emphasis of this month's moon energy cycle is on foundations that education creates. The focus of opening doors for advancement through education will become stronger from March 15th until the day before the full moon March 27th.

New Moon 13th

Unbalancing of the chakra: Crown Chakra

Emotional results: Not feeling good enough or measuring up, depression, loss of motivation

Physical results: Headaches, migraines, insomnia, eye tension, exhaustion, forgetfulness, learning disability

Spiritual results: Yearning for more information and connection

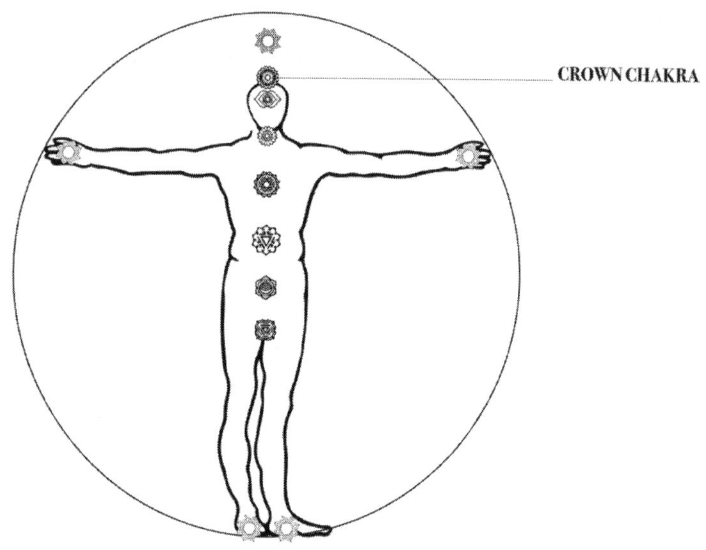

Remedies:

- Movement: Massaging of acupressure points between the lower shoulder blades
- Aromatherapy: Rose, lavender, thyme, oregano, lily of the valley, pine essential oils

- Body: Exposure to sunshine
- Sound therapy: Wind chimes, sounds with movement
- Journal exercise: Write a list of the areas in life that you have excelled in and where you plan to excel

Growth opportunity:

- Take time to read, listen to webinars or attend classes

Full Moon 28th

Remedy:

- Body: Green juices (containing kale or spinach) mangos or persimmons, seafood diet

Mantras

I am opening my mind to new levels, new possibilities and new beliefs about myself and the world around me.

Or

I attract the knowledge and wisdom that I seek. Information flows to me through unexpected sources. All that I seek I find.

April

THE PINK MOON

The emphasis of this month's moon energy cycle is on joy. The focus of aligning and outcomes of joy will become stronger on the April 15th and stay until 3 days before the super moon on the 24th.

New Moon 12th

Unbalancing of the chakra: Third Eye Chakra

Emotional results: No tolerance, irritability, lack of imagination, lack of intuition, easily swayed from truth

Physical results: Allergies, emotional swings, pancreatic issues/craving sweets, mouth sores, muscle tension, sluggish spleen

Spiritual results: Not wanting to connect with other, avoiding the truth

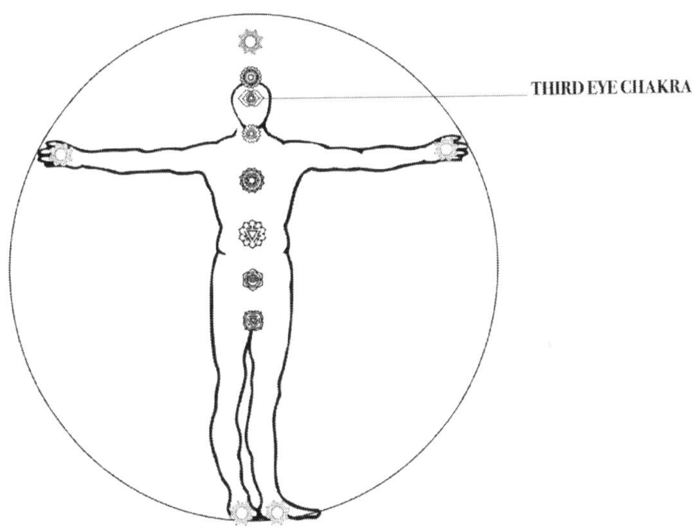

Remedies:

- Movement: Massaging of acupressure points beneath the sternum
- Aromatherapy: Cedar wood, sandalwood, cypress essential oils

- Body: Magnesium supplement
- Sound therapy: Tuning fork 4160C
- Journal exercise: Daily gratitude list

Growth opportunity:

- Take time to indulge in the things that you find pleasure in and pass that on to others

Full Super Moon 27th

Remedies:

- Movement: Dancing, Tai chi, repetitive movement
- Aromatherapy: Bath using Epsom salts and plumeria essential oils
- Body: Teas, orange pekoe, turmeric, any type of tea with clove and cinnamon

Mantras

My life is being surrounded in love, my life is being surrounded in joy, I experience the harmony of having love and joy in my life.

Or

I bring the energy of joy to my home, to my work and to my everyday life in every way.

May

THE FLOWER MOON

The emphasis of this month's moon energy cycle is on decisiveness. The focus on decision making and the ability to follow your heart will become stronger on May 14th until 3 days prior to the super moon on May 23rd.

New Moon 11th

Unbalancing of the chakra: Heart Chakra

Emotional results: Low self-worth, giving but not receiving, loneliness, neediness, defensiveness

Physical results: Muscle tension, skeletal alignment, blood pressure or circulation issues, lung related issue, congestion of breast tissue

Spiritual results: No hope, no vision for the future

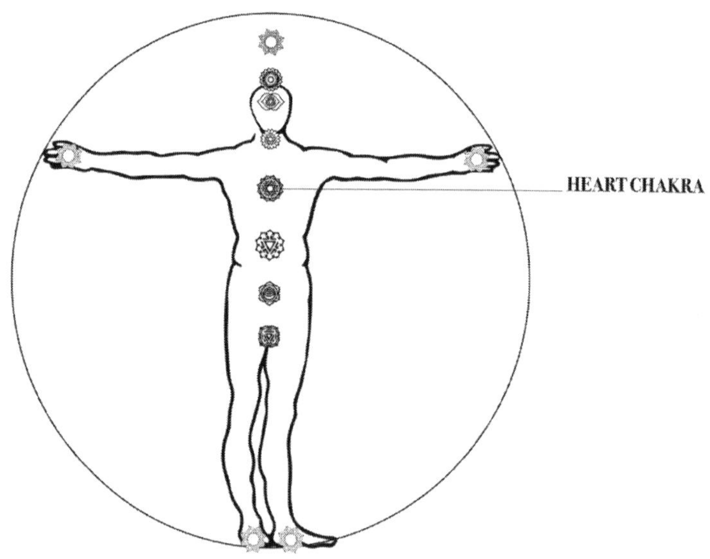

Remedies:

- Movement: Massaging of acupressure points under arm within the arm pit
- Aromatherapy: Rose, neroli essential oils

- Body: Milk thistle or parsley supplements
- Sound therapy: Ocean waves
- Journal exercise: List the decisions you have made over the past year that created forward movement

Growth opportunity:

- Take the time to finalize decisions you have been putting off by following your heart. The universe will support your decision with the super moon that is coming

Super Full Moon 26th

Remedy:

- Movement: Exercise, lots of it, gets of the monkey brain

Mantras

I am excited to bring in new opportunities, I am aligning to open doorways that are exactly what I want.
I am succeeding and exceeding in my dreams and goals.

Or

I am making strong decisions that bring me fulfillment and success in life.

June

THE STRAWBERRY MOON

The emphasis of this month's moon energy cycle is on releasing. The focus on releasing and purging the emotions that no longer serve you becomes stronger on June 13th until 3 days prior to the super moon on June 21st.

New Moon 10th

Unbalancing of the chakra: Root Chakra

Emotional results: Boundary issues, no willpower, loss of sense of success

Physical results: Joint issues of knees and feet, edema, digestive problems, colon problems, liver inflammation, auto immune

Spiritual results: Demanding, loss of patience

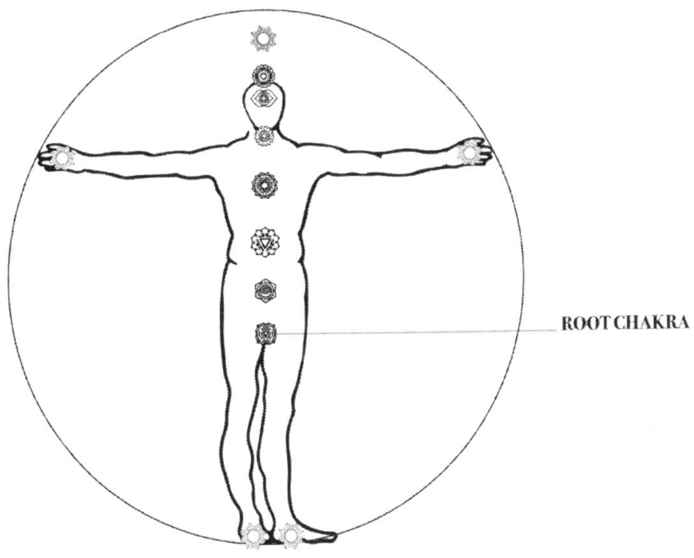

Remedies:

- Movement: Massaging of acupressure points top of neck, base of skull in the C2 area of spinal cord

- Aromatherapy: Myrrh, cypress or wintergreen essential oils
- Body: Vitamin D and E supplements
- Sound therapy: Chopin concertos
- Journal exercise: Deciding in your life what serves you and what does not and learning to release

Balanced Chakra Opportunity:

- Organizing, donating and balancing emotional energy through purging

Full Super Moon 24th

Remedy:

- Body: Chakra balancing meditations

Mantras

My life is in abundance, I am releasing all that is not serving me, creating a balance in my energy.

Or

All that I need is given to me, all that I desire is in my possession and I freely release any obstacles in my life.

July

THE BUCK MOON

The emphasis of this month's moon energy cycle is on empowerment. The focus on the belief in one's own self for empowerment will become stronger on the 13th of March until 1.5 days prior to the full moon on the 22nd.

New Moon 10th

Unbalancing of the chakra: Solar Plexus Chakra

Emotional results: Feeling left out, disconnected, alone, non-acceptance, bullied

Physical results: Stomach issues, acidity, kidney, liver, gallbladder

Spiritual results: Doubt, fear, imposter syndrome

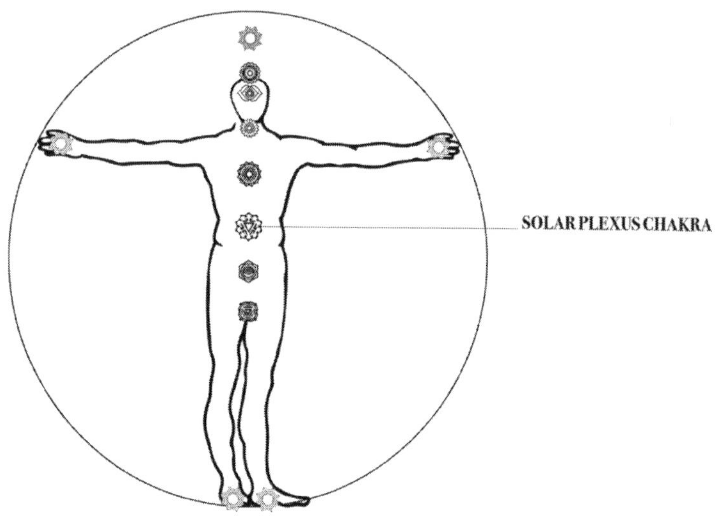

Remedies:

- Movement: Massaging of acupressure points on the ear lobes
- Aromatherapy: Bergamot, citronella, fir balsam, patchouli, verbena essential oils
- Body: Potassium, echinacea supplement

- Sound therapy: Waterfalls, trickling brooks, fountains, rain
- Journal exercise: Write a gratitude list for all your challenges in life that have made you stronger

Growth opportunity:

- Challenge yourself and find an area in life that will expand your success where you have had fear before

Full Moon 24th

Remedies:

- Movement: Long walks surrounded by nature, sports activity with others
- Sound therapy: Nature sounds

Mantras

I am opening my mind to new levels, new possibilities, and new beliefs about myself and the world around me.

Or

I am blessed with being me, the perfect me who is exactly who I am supposed to be.

August

THE STURGEON MOON

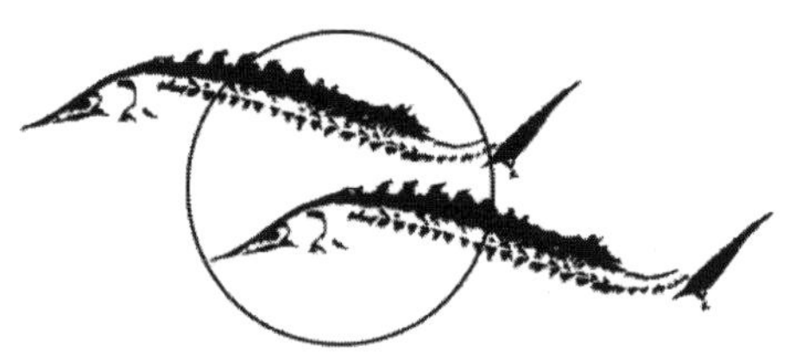

The emphasis of this month's moon energy cycle is on flexibility of the mind. The focus on opening your mind to new beliefs and new ideas will become stronger on the 11th of August until one day before the full moon on the 21th.

New Moon 8th

Unbalancing of the chakras: Crown & Hand Chakras

Emotional results: Defensive, territorial, feeling of being used

Physical results: Headache, dizziness, fatigue, low immune system, low thyroid, stiff muscles and joints

Spiritual results: Feeling stuck, sluggish

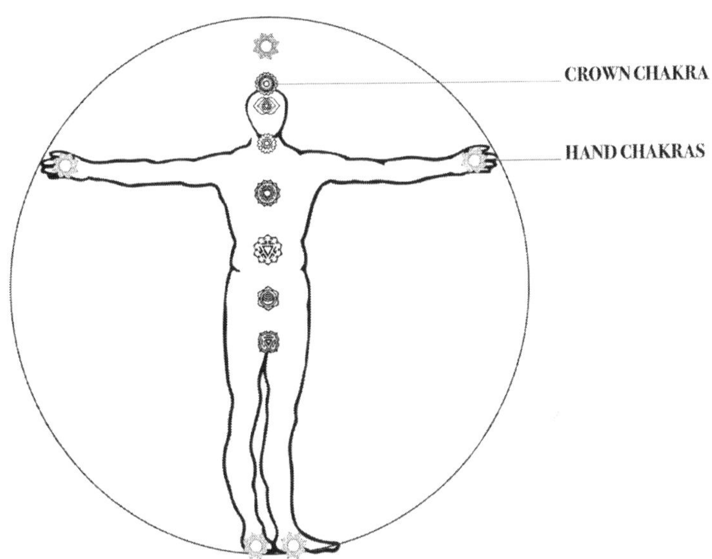

Remedies:

- Movement: Massaging of acupressure points in the base of the palms
- Aromatherapy: Anise star, camphor, hemp, wintergreen essential oils
- Body: Valerian root tea

- Sound therapy: Ocean waves

Growth opportunity:

- Explore your creative energy through art, problem solving, or organization. Try using other peoples' ideas and beliefs, allow criticism to expand your creativity

Full Moon 22nd

Remedies:

- Movement: Travel or new surroundings
- Body: Massage therapy

Mantras

I am accepted, loved, and respected for who I am, who I will be and who I desire to be.

Or

I am allowing new thoughts, new ideas, new beliefs to benefit my mind, body, and soul.

September

THE CORN MOON

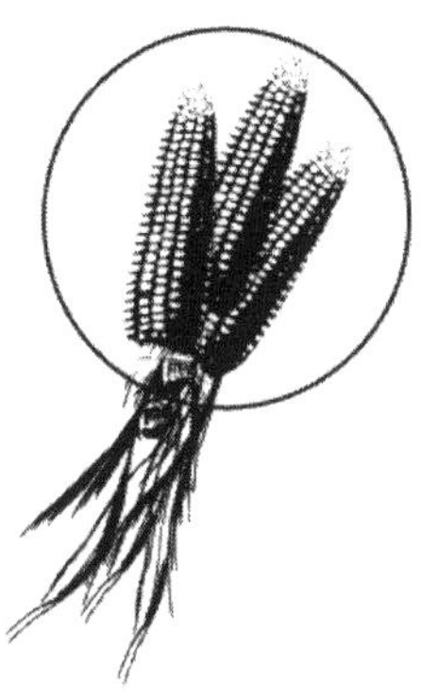

The emphasis of this month's moon energy cycle is on alignment. The focus on alignment and synchronicity will become stronger on 10th of September until 1 day prior to the full moon on the 19th.

New Moon 7th

Unbalancing of the chakras: Root, Heart & Throat Chakras

Emotional results: Impatience, scheduling anxiety, short temper, resentful

Physical results: Blood flow issues, bruising, sprains, increased allergies, hormonal imbalances

Spiritual results: Feeling lack of control

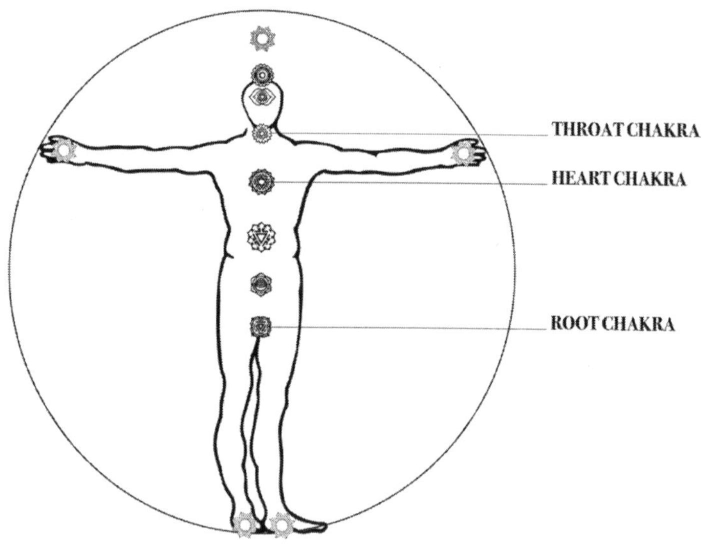

Remedies:

- Movement: Massaging of acupressure points behind the knees and ankles
- Aromatherapy: Cedar wood, cypress, myrtle essential oils

- Body: Vitamin C and B's supplements
- Sound therapy: Mozart concertos

Growth opportunities:

- Building of faith and trust through acknowledging daily that you have received what you desired
- Allowing to receive when others are giving to you

Full Moon 20th

Remedies:

- Body: Relaxation meditations, additional sleep and rest

Mantras

My life is in alignment, open to receiving all the gifts and blessings the universe has to offer me.

Or

My life flows with ease and grace, coming together effortlessly.

October

THE HUNTER MOON

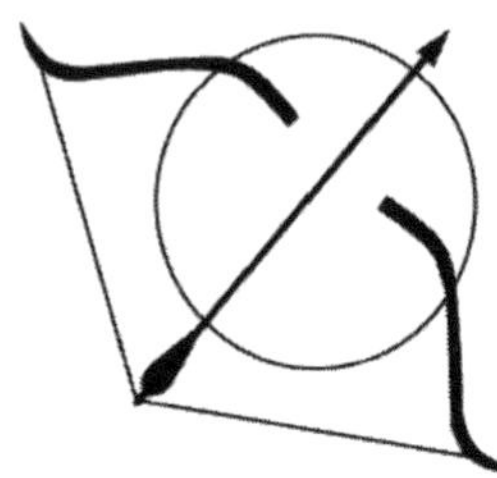

The emphasis of this month's moon energy cycle is on explorations. The focus on new experiences and exploring new connections will become stronger on Oct 9th until one day prior to the full moon on the 19th.

New Moon 6th

Unbalancing of the chakra: Higher Self Chakra

Emotional results: Melancholy, neediness in attention

Physical results: Lymphatic and toxicity issues

Spiritual results: Feeling of Loss

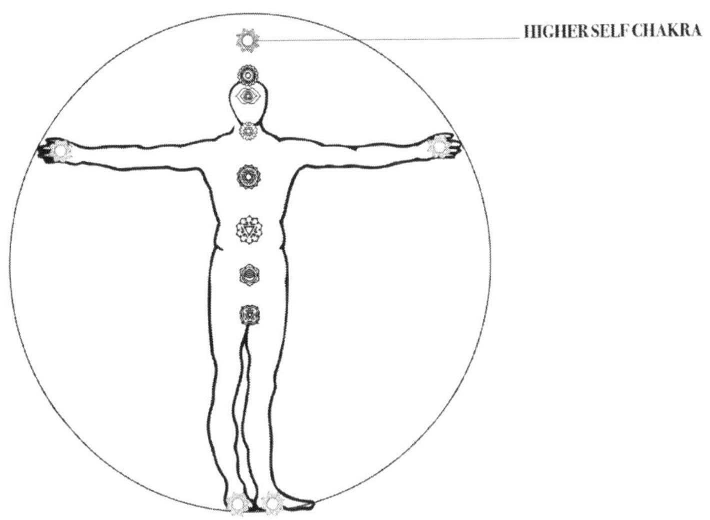

Remedies:

- Movement: Massaging of acupressure points behind the ears, base of skull bone
- Aromatherapy: Cypress or eucalyptus essential oils
- Body: Clove and spiced teas
- Sound therapy: Tuning fork 4096C

Growth opportunity:

- Day trips, new environments, new experiences, a change from the everyday at least 3 times during this moon cycle

Full Moon 20th

Remedies:

- Movement: Laughing, playfulness
- Sound therapy: Sound of others laughing

Mantras

I am exploring the world around me, it offers me comfort, nurturing and expansion for my soul, I am balanced and complete.

Or

I allow the universe to gift me the wisdom and knowledge to move ahead into the unknown.

November

THE BEAVER MOON

The emphasis of this month's moon energy cycle is of the heart. The focus of empathy and nurturing will become stronger on 7th of November until 3 days prior to the super moon on the 16th.

New Moon 4th

Unbalancing of the chakras: Heart & Sacral Chakras

Emotional results: Sadness, lack of joy, no tolerance

Physical results: Lungs, liver, stomach issues, slow digestion, allergies, hormones unbalanced, depression, sinus problems

Spiritual results: Feeling trapped, desperate

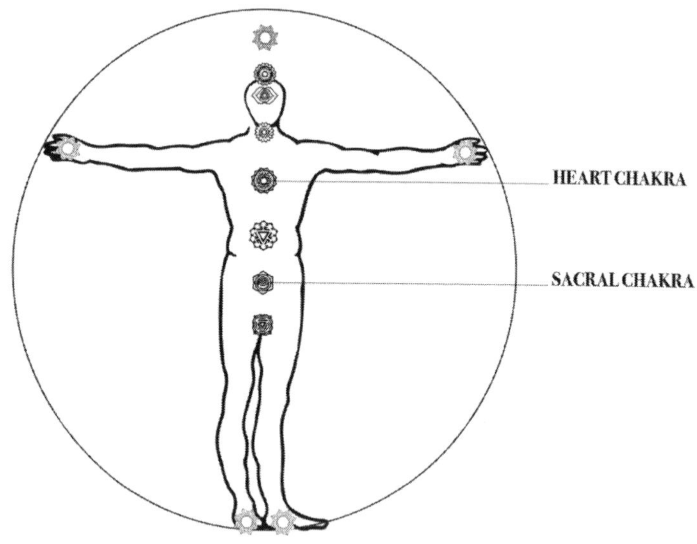

Remedies:

- Movement: Massaging of acupressure points on the balls of the feet below the toes
- Aromatherapy: Clementine, fragonia, ginger, geranium, jasmine, magnolia, patchouli, rose, ylang ylang essential oils

- Body: Magnesium, vitamin B's and C supplements
- Sound therapy: Tchaikovsky concertos

Growth opportunities:

- What can you say or do to improve another person's situation
- Give to others what they desire not what you desire to give

Super Full Moon 19th

Remedies:

- Mind: Being present to those around you
- Body: Sea salt bath for cleansing
- Sound therapy: Listening to the sounds of nature

Mantras

My chakras are balanced and aligned, giving and receiving the love and joy from all those that touch my life. Every life I touch, I spread joy and love.

Or

The universe is nurturing me allowing me to experience love, allowing me to heal my heart.

December

THE COLD MOON

The emphasis of this month's moon energy cycle is on connection. The focus of feeling purpose and valued by others will become stronger on the 7th of December until 3 days prior to the super full moon on the 16th.

New Moon 4th

Unbalancing of the chakras: Third Eye & Root Chakras

Emotional results: Increased sex drive, needing attention, demanding, low self-esteem

Physical results: Nervous system, skin conditions

Spiritual results: Indecisiveness, disconnected, nonproductive

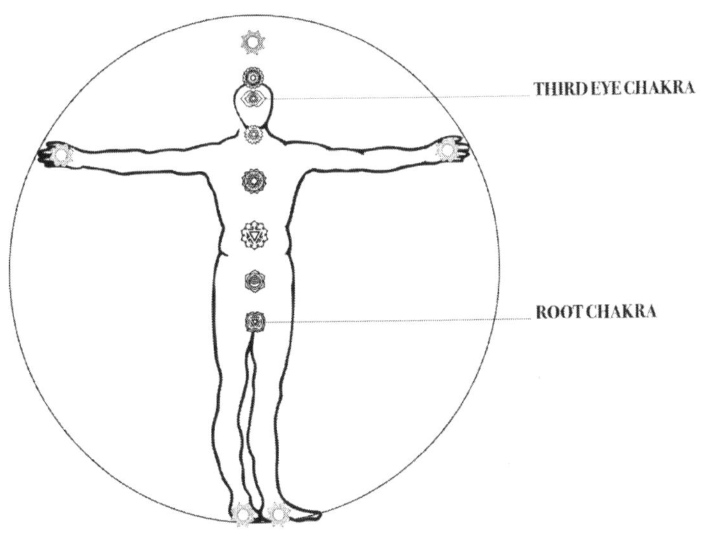

Remedies:

- Movement: Massaging of acupressure points along the mid interior forearm
- Aromatherapy: Lavender, neroli, spikenard essential oils

- Body: Chamomile tea, nutmeg spice, zinc supplement
- Sound therapy: Tuning fork 4225c
- Journal exercise: List the people in your life and how you contribute to each one

Growth opportunity:

- Throughout your day notice when something is easy and pleasurable. Realize the enjoyment you get out of certain tasks, how it contributes to other people's lives and how it contributes to yours

Super Full Moon 19th

Remedies:

- Body: Massage therapy, sea salt baths
- Sound therapy: Rhythmic drumming

Mantras

I am a puzzle piece, one of many, I fit, I belong, I have a purpose to help create a beautiful picture.

Or

I know my purpose deep down inside, I allow it to emerge, I allow it to show itself, I allow it to guide me.

THE ECLIPSES

LUNAR AND SOLAR

SOLAR ECLIPSES

A solar eclipse occurs when the sun, moon and Earth's alignment coincide with a new moon. A portion of the Earth is engulfed in a shadow cast by the moon which can partially block sunlight. A total eclipse is when the sun is blocked by the moon. A partial or annular eclipse is when only part of the sun is blocked.

July 10th, Annular Eclipse

Visibility: The eclipse will be visible through much of Europe, much of Asia, North/West Africa, much of North America, Atlantic, the Arctic.

Effects: This eclipse amplifies the energy of creativity and resolution. Best time to complete projects and begin new ones.

Where: The effects of the energy will be experienced heavier in the areas of Northern Europe, Eastern Asia and North American continent.

When: The energies will last from July 7th to July 18th.

December 4th, Total Solar Eclipse

Visibility: The eclipse will be visible in South Australia, Southern continent of Africa, South America, Pacific, Atlantic, Indian Ocean, Antarctica.

Effects: This eclipse amplifies communications, completions, resolutions and abundance. Best time for negotiations, starting a family and alignment of new ventures.

Where: Energy is affected everywhere, but heavier in the South America continent, Eastern Asia, Middle East.

When: The energies will last from November 30th to Dec 8th.

LUNAR ECLIPSES

Lunar eclipses occur when the sun, Earth and moon are closely aligned, and the Earth is between the sun and the moon. The moon then enters into the Earth's shadow creating the effects of the eclipse. The energy of the moon changes for a short period of time causing an energy disruption.

May 26th, Lunar Eclipse

Visibility: The eclipse will be visible in areas of Southeast Asia, all of Australia, all of Oceania, most of Alaska, Canada, all of the lower 48 states, Hawaii, and most of South America.

Effects: This eclipse will affect matters of heart and completion of projects, contracts, and legal settlements. It is best to hold off on any decision making or commitments during this time period.

Where: All areas will be affected but heavier in European countries and the Eastern part of Asia.

When: The energy will last for a period of 5 days from the 25th to the 29th.

November 19th, Lunar Eclipse

Visibility: This is a partial eclipse that will be seen from much of Europe, much of Asia, Australia, North/West Africa, North America, South America, Pacific, Atlantic, Indian Ocean and the Arctic.

Effects: This eclipse affects communications, connections, alignments, defiance and disagreements. Events with family and friends, and negotiations need special effort to keep balanced during this time period.

Where: The energy will be heavier in the areas of Middle East, Russia, New Zealand, New Guinea, Baltic States, and South Africa.

When: The energies will last for a 3 day period from 18th till 21st.

ORRERY GLASGOW, UK

THE PLANETS

MERCURY, VENUS, EARTH, MARS, JUPITER, SATURN, URANUS, NEPTUNE, PLUTO

THE ENERGY OF OUR PLANETS

Mercury, I think

Mercury contributes the energy of our 5 major senses, communication and intelligence. The planet connects to our nervous system, thyroid, and balance of minerals in the body except for calcium.

Venus, I love

Venus contributes to the energy of love, balance and harmony. The planet connects to dermis, epidermis, and the pancreas.

Mars, I act

Mars contributes to the energy of passion, drive, determination and conflict. The planet connects to red blood cell count and sexual organs.

Jupiter, I grow

Jupiter contributes to the energy of encouragement, wisdom, curiosity, inspiration and passion. The planet connects to the digestive system, saliva glands, kidneys, liver and toxification.

Saturn, I achieve

Saturn contributes to the energy of law and order, rules and boundaries. The planet connects to the skeletal system and calcium absorption.

Uranus, I evolve

Uranus contributes to the energy of the unexpected, innovation, freedom and rebellion. The planet connects to the respiratory system.

Neptune, I dream

Neptune contributes to the energy of intuition, inspirational energy, creativity, illusions and delusions. The planet connects to the circulatory system, endocrine, lymphatic systems and joints.

Pluto, I am empowered

Pluto contributes to the energy of power, strength and elemental forces. The planet connects to the immune system and reproductive system.

THE RETROGRADES

PLANETS IN MOTION

MERCURY

Retrograde dates:

January 30 – February 21st

May 30 – June 23rd

September 27 – October 18th

Dormant state:

February 7 - 11th
Jupiter's energy influences curiosity, inspiration, and increase in passion.

June 8 - 12th
Saturn's energy influences law and order, rules and boundaries.

October 4 - 8th
Neptune's energy influences intuition, inspirational creativity, illusions and delusions.

Mercury rules over the energy of communication, intelligence, and awareness. It is never more than 28 degrees from the sun and takes only 88 days to complete its orbit of the sun. This planet travels around the sun 4 times faster than the Earth and will go into retrograde 3 times per year. Retrograde is a word with Latin origins meaning to travel backwards, however it is an optical illusion. The actual retrograde effect occurs when a planet's energy is blocked due to the position of the sun in its orbital phase. Mercury goes into retrograde when it appears behind the sun and coming up behind the Earth each time it passes the Earth on its orbital transition.

When Mercury is in orbit, there is a point when the sun's position is between the Earth and Mercury. Mercury's energy weakens on the Earth's plane, allowing other planets that are in direct alignment with Earth to become stronger. The planet Mercury has direct effect on the strength of magnesium, manganese, copper, iodine, and selenium. During the 4.5 days, that the planet travels behind the sun, these elements are at their weakest points because Mercury's energy enters into a dormant stage on our planet being blocked by the sun. Weakened elements would explain why technology containing cooper becomes a source of frustration when it does not keep up with the workload. During the latter parts of the retrograde stage, the energy builds back into full strength on planet Earth.

Mercury retrograde has a greater effect on those with emotional issues of communications or intelligence and those with issues of low mineral content in the body.

MERCURY

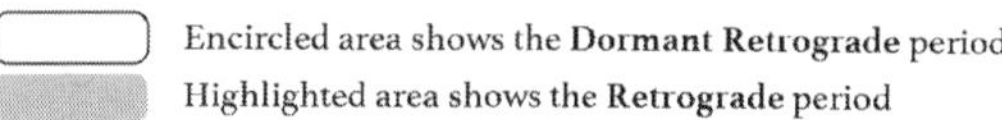

Encircled area shows the **Dormant Retrograde** period

Highlighted area shows the **Retrograde** period

JANUARY	1 2 3 4 5 6 7 8 9 10 11 12 13 14 15 16 17 18 19 20 21 22 23 24 25 26 27 28 29 30 31
FEBRUARY	1 2 3 4 5 6 7 8 9 10 11 12 13 14 15 16 17 18 19 20 21 22 23 24 25 26 27 28
MARCH	1 2 3 4 5 6 7 8 9 10 11 12 13 14 15 16 17 18 19 20 21 22 23 24 25 26 27 28 29 30 31
APRIL	1 2 3 4 5 6 7 8 9 10 11 12 13 14 15 16 17 18 19 20 21 22 23 24 25 26 27 28 29 30
MAY	1 2 3 4 5 6 7 8 9 10 11 12 13 14 15 16 17 18 19 20 21 22 23 24 25 26 27 28 29 30 31
JUNE	1 2 3 4 5 6 7 8 9 10 11 12 13 14 15 16 17 18 19 20 21 22 23 24 25 26 27 28 29 30
JULY	1 2 3 4 5 6 7 8 9 10 11 12 13 14 15 16 17 18 19 20 21 22 23 24 25 26 27 28 29 30 31
AUGUST	1 2 3 4 5 6 7 8 9 10 11 12 13 14 15 16 17 18 19 20 21 22 23 24 25 26 27 28 29 30 31
SEPTEMBER	1 2 3 4 5 6 7 8 9 10 11 12 13 14 15 16 17 18 19 20 21 22 23 24 25 26 27 28 29 30
OCTOBER	1 2 3 4 5 6 7 8 9 10 11 12 13 14 15 16 17 18 19 20 21 22 23 24 25 26 27 28 29 30 31
NOVEMBER	1 2 3 4 5 6 7 8 9 10 11 12 13 14 15 16 17 18 19 20 21 22 23 24 25 26 27 28 29 30
DECEMBER	1 2 3 4 5 6 7 8 9 10 11 12 13 14 15 16 17 18 19 20 21 22 23 24 25 26 27 28 29 30 31

VENUS

Retrograde date:

December 19 - January 29th, 2022

Dormant state:

December 28 – January 5th, 2022

Saturn's energy influences law and order, rules and boundaries increase.

The energy of Venus encourages love and abundance. The orbit of Venus is 255 days around the sun. The retrograde period for Venus is every 18 months for 42 days. Venus is traveling faster than the Earth but manages to have the least amount of time in retrograde. When Venus and Earth are in orbit around the sun, there is a point when the sun is between Earth and Venus, creating a dormant period of Venus' energy for 3 days. While Venus is dormant, Saturn's energy of law, order, rules, and boundaries increases.

Venus supports the sensory perceptions of touch, the dermis and epidermis, sugar levels in the body, insulin production, and carbohydrates digestion. You may notice that you need more support during the retrograde if you have sensitivity in these areas. During the first 9 days of this retrograde, connectivity issues with a loved one and plans falling through both personal and business may be occurring. The following 3 days during the dormant stage, there will be an increase of rules and boundaries. In the last period, while Venus' energy is increasing and coming into balance again, new beginnings and opportunities to sort through issues blocking love and abundance begin to appear.

VENUS

 Encircled area shows the **Dormant Retrograde** period

Highlighted area shows the **Retrograde** period

JANUARY	1 2 3 4 5 6 7 8 9 10 11 12 13 14 15 16 17 18 19 20 21 22 23 24 25 26 27 28 29 30 31
FEBRUARY	1 2 3 4 5 6 7 8 9 10 11 12 13 14 15 16 17 18 19 20 21 22 23 24 25 26 27 28
MARCH	1 2 3 4 5 6 7 8 9 10 11 12 13 14 15 16 17 18 19 20 21 22 23 24 25 26 27 28 29 30 31
APRIL	1 2 3 4 5 6 7 8 9 10 11 12 13 14 15 16 17 18 19 20 21 22 23 24 25 26 27 28 29 30
MAY	1 2 3 4 5 6 7 8 9 10 11 12 13 14 15 16 17 18 19 20 21 22 23 24 25 26 27 28 29 30 31
JUNE	1 2 3 4 5 6 7 8 9 10 11 12 13 14 15 16 17 18 19 20 21 22 23 24 25 26 27 28 29 30
JULY	1 2 3 4 5 6 7 8 9 10 11 12 13 14 15 16 17 18 19 20 21 22 23 24 25 26 27 28 29 30 31
AUGUST	1 2 3 4 5 6 7 8 9 10 11 12 13 14 15 16 17 18 19 20 21 22 23 24 25 26 27 28 29 30 31
SEPTEMBER	1 2 3 4 5 6 7 8 9 10 11 12 13 14 15 16 17 18 19 20 21 22 23 24 25 26 27 28 29 30
OCTOBER	1 2 3 4 5 6 7 8 9 10 11 12 13 14 15 16 17 18 19 20 21 22 23 24 25 26 27 28 29 30 31
NOVEMBER	1 2 3 4 5 6 7 8 9 10 11 12 13 14 15 16 17 18 19 20 21 22 23 24 25 26 27 28 29 30
DECEMBER	1 2 3 4 5 6 7 8 9 10 11 12 13 14 15 16 17 18 19 20 21 22 23 24 25 26 27 28 29 30 31
JANUARY 2022	1 2 3 4 5 6 7 8 9 10 11 12 13 14 15 16 17 18 19 20 21 22 23 24 25 26 27 28 29 30 31

MARS

There is no retrograde for Mars in 2021. The next retrograde occurs in 2022.

Retrograde date:

October 30, 2022 – January 12, 2023

JUPITER

Retrograde date:

June 20 - October 17th

Dormant state:

July 8 – 15th
Neptune's energy influences intuition, inspiration, creativity, illusions and delusions.

The energy of Jupiter encourages wisdom, curiosity, inspiration, and passions. The orbit of Jupiter is 11.86 years around the sun. The retrograde period is 4 months and happens about every 9 months. The Earth travels almost 12 times faster around the sun than Jupiter, which causes the longer retrograde period. When Jupiter and the Earth are in orbit around the sun, there is a point when the sun is between the Earth and Jupiter, creating a dormant period of Jupiter's energy for 8 days. When Jupiter's energy weakens during this dormant period, Neptune's energy of intuition, inspirational energy, creativity, illusions, and delusions increases.

Jupiter supports the kidneys, liver, and detoxification. During the retrograde period you will notice you need more support if you have sensitivity in these areas. Jupiter directly affects the growth of spiritual and physical knowledge. Jupiter also affects the growth of plants. Certain species will slow down their growth during retrograde. During the first three weeks of the retrograde period, you may find yourself questioning faith and pathways in life, opening the door for Neptune to expand your intuition and inspiration. In the last 9 weeks of this retrograde, the energy of Jupiter begins to increase and rebalance.

JUPITER

Encircled area shows the **Dormant Retrograde** period

Highlighted area shows the **Retrograde** period

JANUARY	1 2 3 4 5 6 7 8 9 10 11 12 13 14 15 16 17 18 19 20 21 22 23 24 25 26 27 28 29 30 31
FEBRUARY	1 2 3 4 5 6 7 8 9 10 11 12 13 14 15 16 17 18 19 20 21 22 23 24 25 26 27 28
MARCH	1 2 3 4 5 6 7 8 9 10 11 12 13 14 15 16 17 18 19 20 21 22 23 24 25 26 27 28 29 30 31
APRIL	1 2 3 4 5 6 7 8 9 10 11 12 13 14 15 16 17 18 19 20 21 22 23 24 25 26 27 28 29 30
MAY	1 2 3 4 5 6 7 8 9 10 11 12 13 14 15 16 17 18 19 20 21 22 23 24 25 26 27 28 29 30 31
JUNE	1 2 3 4 5 6 7 8 9 10 11 12 13 14 15 16 17 18 19 [Retrograde: 20 21 22 23 24 25 26 27 28 29 30]
JULY	[Retrograde: 1 2 3 4 5 6 7] [Dormant Retrograde: 8 9 10 11 12 13 14 15] [Retrograde: 16 17 18 19 20 21 22 23 24 25 26 27 28 29 30 31]
AUGUST	[Retrograde: 1 2 3 4 5 6 7 8 9 10 11 12 13 14 15 16 17 18 19 20 21 22 23 24 25 26 27 28 29 30 31]
SEPTEMBER	[Retrograde: 1 2 3 4 5 6 7 8 9 10 11 12 13 14 15 16 17 18 19 20 21 22 23 24 25 26 27 28 29 30]
OCTOBER	[Retrograde: 1 2 3 4 5 6 7 8 9 10 11 12 13 14 15 16 17] 18 19 20 21 22 23 24 25 26 27 28 29 30 31
NOVEMBER	1 2 3 4 5 6 7 8 9 10 11 12 13 14 15 16 17 18 19 20 21 22 23 24 25 26 27 28 29 30
DECEMBER	1 2 3 4 5 6 7 8 9 10 11 12 13 14 15 16 17 18 19 20 21 22 23 24 25 26 27 28 29 30 31

SATURN

Retrograde date:

May 23 - October 11th

Dormant state:

July 14 - August 5th

Venus' energy influences love, balance and harmony.

The energy of Saturn is of law, order, rules, and boundaries. The orbit of Saturn is 29.5 years around the sun. The retrograde period is 140 days, about every 12 months. The Earth travels 29 times faster than Saturn around the sun causing the retrograde period to be longer.

When Saturn and Earth are in orbit around the sun, there is a point when the sun is between the Earth and Saturn, creating a dormant period. When Saturn's energy weakens during this dormant period, Venus' energy of love, balance and harmony increases.

Saturn supports the colon and the pituitary gland. During retrograde periods you will need more support if you have sensitivity in these areas. Saturn directly affects karma (cause and effect). During the 2.5 weeks, you will notice a bit more of a struggle to keep things on track. When Venus energy comes in, you will be able to apply more patience and harmony to your day. In the final period of this retrograde, when Saturn starts to rebalance the energy on Earth, you will find the need to enforce more boundaries within certain relationships and personal habits.

SATURN

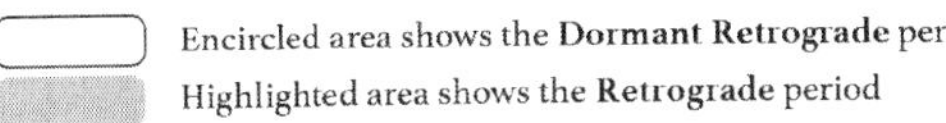

Month	Days
JANUARY	1 2 3 4 5 6 7 8 9 10 11 12 13 14 15 16 17 18 19 20 21 22 23 24 25 26 27 28 29 30 31
FEBRUARY	1 2 3 4 5 6 7 8 9 10 11 12 13 14 15 16 17 18 19 20 21 22 23 24 25 26 27 28
MARCH	1 2 3 4 5 6 7 8 9 10 11 12 13 14 15 16 17 18 19 20 21 22 23 24 25 26 27 28 29 30 31
APRIL	1 2 3 4 5 6 7 8 9 10 11 12 13 14 15 16 17 18 19 20 21 22 23 24 25 26 27 28 29 30
MAY	1 2 3 4 5 6 7 8 9 10 11 12 13 14 15 16 17 18 19 20 21 22 23 24 25 26 27 28 29 30 31
JUNE	1 2 3 4 5 6 7 8 9 10 11 12 13 14 15 16 17 18 19 20 21 22 23 24 25 26 27 28 29 30
JULY	1 2 3 4 5 6 7 8 9 10 11 12 13 14 15 16 17 18 19 20 21 22 23 24 25 26 27 28 29 30 31
AUGUST	1 2 3 4 5 6 7 8 9 10 11 12 13 14 15 16 17 18 19 20 21 22 23 24 25 26 27 28 29 30 31
SEPTEMBER	1 2 3 4 5 6 7 8 9 10 11 12 13 14 15 16 17 18 19 20 21 22 23 24 25 26 27 28 29 30
OCTOBER	1 2 3 4 5 6 7 8 9 10 11 12 13 14 15 16 17 18 19 20 21 22 23 24 25 26 27 28 29 30 31
NOVEMBER	1 2 3 4 5 6 7 8 9 10 11 12 13 14 15 16 17 18 19 20 21 22 23 24 25 26 27 28 29 30
DECEMBER	1 2 3 4 5 6 7 8 9 10 11 12 13 14 15 16 17 18 19 20 21 22 23 24 25 26 27 28 29 30 31

URANUS

Retrograde date:

January 14 - August 20th

Dormant state:

February 19 - March 7th
Mars' energy influences passion, drive, determination and conflict.

The energy of Uranus is of the unexpected, innovation, freedom and rebellion. Uranus' orbit period around the sun is 84 years. The retrograde period is yearly and lasts for about 148 days. When Uranus is in orbit, there is a point when the sun's position is between Uranus and the Earth. Blocking Uranus' energy and weakening it on the Earth's plane. During that time, it allows Mars' energy of passion, drive, and determination, and conflict to strengthen for 25 days.

Uranus supports the nervous system. During a retrograde, people with stressful lives will experience shortened tempers, lack of patience, tremors, acidic bodies, low estrogen levels and intestinal problems more than usual. The first 34 days of the retrograde, you may experience a slowing of creativity, problem solving, and increased frustration. The next 25 days during the dormant stage, determination and drive set in. As Uranus' energy comes back to rebalance during the completion of the retrograde, creativity and freedom will slowly emerge coming back to normal.

URANUS

Encircled area shows the **Dormant Retrograde** period

Highlighted area shows the **Retrograde** period

JANUARY	1 2 3 4 5 6 7 8 9 10 11 12 13 14 15 16 17 18 19 20 21 22 23 24 25 26 27 28 29 30 31
FEBRUARY	1 2 3 4 5 6 7 8 9 10 11 12 13 14 15 16 17 18 19 20 21 22 23 24 25 26 27 28
MARCH	1 2 3 4 5 6 7 8 9 10 11 12 13 14 15 16 17 18 19 20 21 22 23 24 25 26 27 28 29 30 31
APRIL	1 2 3 4 5 6 7 8 9 10 11 12 13 14 15 16 17 18 19 20 21 22 23 24 25 26 27 28 29 30
MAY	1 2 3 4 5 6 7 8 9 10 11 12 13 14 15 16 17 18 19 20 21 22 23 24 25 26 27 28 29 30 31
JUNE	1 2 3 4 5 6 7 8 9 10 11 12 13 14 15 16 17 18 19 20 21 22 23 24 25 26 27 28 29 30
JULY	1 2 3 4 5 6 7 8 9 10 11 12 13 14 15 16 17 18 19 20 21 22 23 24 25 26 27 28 29 30 31
AUGUST	1 2 3 4 5 6 7 8 9 10 11 12 13 14 15 16 17 18 19 20 21 22 23 24 25 26 27 28 29 30 31
SEPTEMBER	1 2 3 4 5 6 7 8 9 10 11 12 13 14 15 16 17 18 19 20 21 22 23 24 25 26 27 28 29 30
OCTOBER	1 2 3 4 5 6 7 8 9 10 11 12 13 14 15 16 17 18 19 20 21 22 23 24 25 26 27 28 29 30 31
NOVEMBER	1 2 3 4 5 6 7 8 9 10 11 12 13 14 15 16 17 18 19 20 21 22 23 24 25 26 27 28 29 30
DECEMBER	1 2 3 4 5 6 7 8 9 10 11 12 13 14 15 16 17 18 19 20 21 22 23 24 25 26 27 28 29 30 31

NEPTUNE

Retrograde date:

June 25 - December 1st

Dormant state:

August 26 - September 14th
Jupiter's energy influences encouragement, curiosity, inspiration, and increase in passion.

The energy of Neptune is intuition, inspiration, creativity, illusions and delusions. The orbit of Neptune is 164.79 years around the sun. It never appears in our sky in the same place within the year. The retrograde period comes yearly and lasts for 158 days. When Neptune and the Earth are in orbit around the sun, there is a point when the sun is between the two, creating a dormant period for Neptune's energy on the Earth for 26 days. When Neptune's energy weakens on the planet during the dormant stage, Jupiter's energy of encouragement, wisdom, curiosity, inspiration and passion strengthens.

Neptune supports the lymphatic system, the pineal gland, the thymus gland, and the spleen. During the retrograde period, you may feel lethargic, exhaustion, and restless sleep. Neptune directly affects the higher aspirations of purpose in life. During the first 63 days of the retrograde, a feeling of uncertainty and indecision comes in. The dormant stage will change viewpoints, open doors to new adventures, and new desires. When Neptune's energy starts to build and rebalance, our spirituality, inner tranquility, and vision become the focus during the final stage.

NEPTUNE

Encircled area shows the **Dormant Retrograde** period

Highlighted area shows the **Retrograde** period

Month	Days
JANUARY	1 2 3 4 5 6 7 8 9 10 11 12 13 14 15 16 17 18 19 20 21 22 23 24 25 26 27 28 29 30 31
FEBRUARY	1 2 3 4 5 6 7 8 9 10 11 12 13 14 15 16 17 18 19 20 21 22 23 24 25 26 27 28
MARCH	1 2 3 4 5 6 7 8 9 10 11 12 13 14 15 16 17 18 19 20 21 22 23 24 25 26 27 28 29 30 31
APRIL	1 2 3 4 5 6 7 8 9 10 11 12 13 14 15 16 17 18 19 20 21 22 23 24 25 26 27 28 29 30
MAY	1 2 3 4 5 6 7 8 9 10 11 12 13 14 15 16 17 18 19 20 21 22 23 24 25 26 27 28 29 30 31
JUNE	1 2 3 4 5 6 7 8 9 10 11 12 13 14 15 16 17 18 19 20 21 22 23 24 25 26 27 28 29 30
JULY	1 2 3 4 5 6 7 8 9 10 11 12 13 14 15 16 17 18 19 20 21 22 23 24 25 26 27 28 29 30 31
AUGUST	1 2 3 4 5 6 7 8 9 10 11 12 13 14 15 16 17 18 19 20 21 22 23 24 25 26 27 28 29 30 31
SEPTEMBER	1 2 3 4 5 6 7 8 9 10 11 12 13 14 15 16 17 18 19 20 21 22 23 24 25 26 27 28 29 30
OCTOBER	1 2 3 4 5 6 7 8 9 10 11 12 13 14 15 16 17 18 19 20 21 22 23 24 25 26 27 28 29 30 31
NOVEMBER	1 2 3 4 5 6 7 8 9 10 11 12 13 14 15 16 17 18 19 20 21 22 23 24 25 26 27 28 29 30
DECEMBER	1 2 3 4 5 6 7 8 9 10 11 12 13 14 15 16 17 18 19 20 21 22 23 24 25 26 27 28 29 30 31

PLUTO

Retrograde date:

April 27 - October 6th

Dormant state:

May 27 - June 20th

Jupiter's energy influences curiosity, inspiration, and increase in passion.

Venus' energy influences love, balance and harmony.

Saturn's energy influences law and order, rules and boundaries increase.

The energy of Pluto is transformation, regeneration, and rebirth. The orbit of Pluto around the sun is 248 years. The retrograde period is yearly, lasting for 5 to 6 months. Pluto has been downgraded and now considered a star; however, it contributes energy to the Earth. When Pluto and the Earth are in orbit around the sun, there is a point when the sun is between the Earth and Pluto, creating a dormant stage for Pluto's energy for a period of 25 days. When Pluto's energy weakens, the energy of 3 planets strengthens, Jupiter, Venus, and Saturn, the "I grow", "I achieve", and "I love energy". These 25 days are golden. A perfect time for vision boards, new goals, renewing commitments or vows.

Pluto supports the heart, circulatory and reproductive organs. During the retrograde period you won't notice much of a change in any of these conditions. The dormant stage, however, you could notice a change in heart rate due to an increase in the desire to complete things and move forward. There is also an increase in fertility. The first 4 weeks of this retrograde a separation of habit, relationships or patterns occur. During the dormant stage the energy to create change is support by new paths. The last phase when the energy is rebuilding and rebalancing connecting to new ideas, purpose and determination strengthens.

PLUTO

Encircled area shows the **Dormant Retrograde** period

Highlighted area shows the **Retrograde** period

Month	Days
JANUARY	1 2 3 4 5 6 7 8 9 10 11 12 13 14 15 16 17 18 19 20 21 22 23 24 25 26 27 28 29 30 31
FEBRUARY	1 2 3 4 5 6 7 8 9 10 11 12 13 14 15 16 17 18 19 20 21 22 23 24 25 26 27 28
MARCH	1 2 3 4 5 6 7 8 9 10 11 12 13 14 15 16 17 18 19 20 21 22 23 24 25 26 27 28 29 30 31
APRIL	1 2 3 4 5 6 7 8 9 10 11 12 13 14 15 16 17 18 19 20 21 22 23 24 25 26 27 28 29 30
MAY	1 2 3 4 5 6 7 8 9 10 11 12 13 14 15 16 17 18 19 20 21 22 23 24 25 26 27 28 29 30 31
JUNE	1 2 3 4 5 6 7 8 9 10 11 12 13 14 15 16 17 18 19 20 21 22 23 24 25 26 27 28 29 30
JULY	1 2 3 4 5 6 7 8 9 10 11 12 13 14 15 16 17 18 19 20 21 22 23 24 25 26 27 28 29 30 31
AUGUST	1 2 3 4 5 6 7 8 9 10 11 12 13 14 15 16 17 18 19 20 21 22 23 24 25 26 27 28 29 30 31
SEPTEMBER	1 2 3 4 5 6 7 8 9 10 11 12 13 14 15 16 17 18 19 20 21 22 23 24 25 26 27 28 29 30
OCTOBER	1 2 3 4 5 6 7 8 9 10 11 12 13 14 15 16 17 18 19 20 21 22 23 24 25 26 27 28 29 30 31
NOVEMBER	1 2 3 4 5 6 7 8 9 10 11 12 13 14 15 16 17 18 19 20 21 22 23 24 25 26 27 28 29 30
DECEMBER	1 2 3 4 5 6 7 8 9 10 11 12 13 14 15 16 17 18 19 20 21 22 23 24 25 26 27 28 29 30 31

THE ENERGY GRIDS

THE EARTH

GRID ALIGNMENTS

Grids are the Earth's energy flow system. They consist of 78 major grids combined with 2144 minor underlying grids. They are connected to each other by planetary meridian points, much like the human body's meridian points. The Earth's grids are formed by combining the tonality in sound waves, the frequency in light waves, and the Earth's gravitational pull creating an energy field. Major energy grids are connected to locations and connect to portals when they open to the Earth's energy. Minor energy grids connect to humans and also create vortexes. Vortexes are created when multiple minor energy grids are layered on top of each other and connect to a major grid, creating an intense energy field.

Our bodies' energy interacts with the environmental energy grids influencing our emotional states. We begin to match the environment's frequency, which creates change leading to opportunities or challenges in our lives. Star alignments, planetary movements, and human emotional patterns can all cause frequency shifts in the grids. Society experiencing strong emotions tied to an event can be seen on the Schumann Resonance. As emotions rise and lower, the emotional frequency affects the underlying minor energy grids. The Schumann Resonance is the measurement of the frequencies of natural harmonics in the planetary electromagnetic fields. The natural resonant frequency of 7.83 Hz of the planet matches the alpha brain wave patterns of healthy human consciousness. During international prayer times, the frequency has risen, causing the emotions of peace and calm to emerge.

During times of civil unrest, the frequency will decrease creating fear, depression, and defensiveness.
Each grid will have a corresponding grid in one of the other four hemispheres to keep the balance of frequencies on the planet. When one changes the interconnected grid will shift.

The use of natural remedies of essential oils of floral or evergreen and repetitive sound waves such as the ocean, chimes, or signing bowls will create a balance in the body's frequencies, negating the effects of shifting girds or traveling to different grids.

North-East Asia And Northern African

Five major energy grids shift in these areas from early April to mid-November due to the alignment of Neptune with Mars.

North-East Asia:
Current energy cooperation, balance, and flexibility

Shifting to the energy of disagreement, defiance, and conflict

Northern Africa:
Current energy of disagreement, defiance and conflict

Shifting to the energy of cooperation, balance, and flexibility

---

Upper Eastern Coast of North America and Western Middle East

Three major energy grids shift in these areas from August till January 2022 due to the alignment of Venus and Jupiter.

Upper Eastern Coast:
Current energy of creativity, developing foundations and security

Shifting to the energy of education and advancements

Western Middle East:
Current energy of education and advancements

Shifting to the energy of creativity developing foundations and security

---

Eastern Europe and Greenland

Three major energy grids shift in these areas from early September till January 2022 due to Mars and Uranus's alignment.

Eastern Europe:
Current energy of innovation, rebellion and progress

Shifting to financial flow and abundance

Greenland:
Current energy of financial flow and abundance

Shifting to innovation, rebellion, and progress

Iceland and Eastern & Southern Australia, New Zealand

Eight major energy grids shift in these areas from early September until January 2022 due to Jupiter and Mars alignment.

Iceland:
Current energy of passion, drive, and determination

Shifting to the energy of wisdom, inspiration, and curiosity

Eastern & Southern Australia and New Zealand:
Current energy of wisdom, inspiration, and curiosity

Shifting to the energy of passion, drive, and determination

Northern China and the Mediterranean

One major energy grid shifts in these areas from early September until January 2022 due to Uranus and Mars position.

Mediterranean:
Current energy of innovation, rebellion, and freedom

Shifting to the energy of passion, drive, determination and conflicting

Northern China:
Current energy of passion, drive, determination and conflict

Shifting to innovation, rebellion, and freedom.

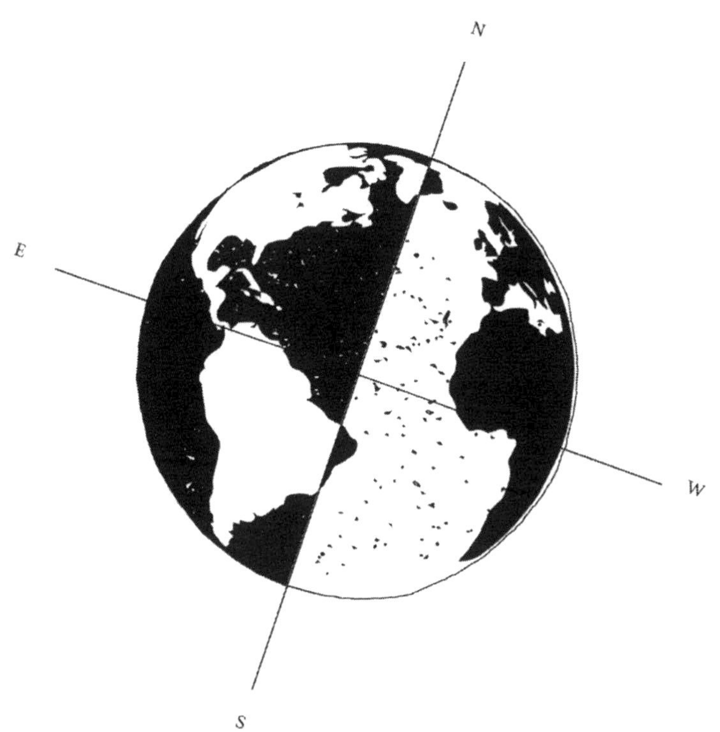

THE SOLSTICES & EQUINOXES

VERNAL, SUMMER, AUTUMNAL, WINTER

SUMMER SOLSTICE

Northern Hemisphere: June 20, 2021
Southern Hemisphere: December 21, 2021

The word solstice has origins from the Latin words "sol," meaning sun and "stitium," meaning still. It is the day with the longest daylight and the shortest period of darkness. The solstice is part of an ancient wisdom. Its traditions celebrate new beginnings each year.

Our bodies react in several different ways to the change in the sun's position. Our nervous system becomes more responsive. The pituitary gland opens up and increases the production of hormones. Our sense of taste changes, and we desire a higher amount of protein. Our DNA's ancient memories prepare us for hunting, gathering, and procreation during the warmer months.

Winter Solstice

Northern Hemisphere: December 21, 2021
Southern Hemisphere: June 20, 2021

The Winter Solstice is also known as the Hibernal (from the word hibernation) Solstice. For a good reason, our bodies react to the shortest day of the year by slowing down our nervous and digestive system. Our lymphatic system increases, and our taste changes to crave more fat in our diet. The wisdom of our body is getting us ready for the long winter months.

Vernal Equinox

Northern Hemisphere: March 20, 2021
Southern Hemisphere: September 22, 2021

Autumnal Equinox

Northern Hemisphere: September 22, 2021
Southern Hemisphere: March 20, 2021

An equinox occurs when the night and the day are the same lengths worldwide. The equinoxes' precession is caused by the differential gravitational forces of the sun and the moon on the Earth. The change in the gravitational pull will affect our bodies—the closer to the equator, the greater the effect.

The effect on the body is the same for both equinoxes and can last up to two weeks:

Low energy
Headaches
Sleep patterns disruption
Sinus problems
Change in sex drive
Appetite changes
Underactive spleen
Weak thymus gland
Onset of depression or anxiety

FLAME & HORSEHEAD NEBULAR IN ORION'S BELT GALAXY

THE STARS

STAR GATES & FENG SHUI

THE STAR GATES

DEER GATE, LION'S GATE, BEAR GATE

PORTALS

Star Gates are portals that connect to the major energy grids on the planet. A portal is similar to a chakra, a transportation vehicle, transporting energy from one place to another, in this case from a star to the Earth.

THE DEER GATE

The Deer Gate opens a portal created by the Earth's alignment to the star Polaris in the constellation Ursa Minor. This gate opens the energy of love and healing for both the physical and emotional bodies. Polaris' alignment to the sun and the Earth in February allows the portal to open for as long as 27 days and as short as 8 days each year. The shifting of the Earth's energy grids affects the portal's energy. This year's energy grids allow the portal's energy to exist from February 6th to February 14th.

The deer represents the removal of obstacles, which is what this portals energy creates for healing. Although not as strong as the other star gates, this one still allows you to access the energy through the heart chakra. The use of sound baths and meditations can amplify the portal's energy to remove the obstacles from your life path.

THE LION'S GATE

The Lion's Gate is the opening of a portal created by the Earth coming into alignment with Sirius, a binary star in the constellation Canis Major and the Belt of Orion, also known as the Three Sister or Three Kings. Orion consists of 3 bright stars, Alnitak, Alnilam, and Mintaka, when in this alignment, they amplify Sirius' energy. This gate is known to align perfectly with the Pyramids of Giza. Civilizations dating back thousands of years have tracked the rising of Sirius to come into alignment with the sun awaiting the magical, mystical powers of this portal's energy of creating abundance.

The energy duration depends on the energy grids on Earth at the time of alignment. It can last as long as 18 days and as short as 2 days. This year the energy will last for 5 days from August 5th to August 10th.

Meditations, positive writing, and affirmations are tools you can use to help align your thoughts to direct this portal's energy for your life's goals.

THE BEAR GATE

The Bear Gate opens a portal created by the Earth's alignment to the star Dubhe in the constellation Ursa Major. This gate opens the energy of wisdom and strength. Dubhe's alignment to the sun and the Earth in October allows the portal to open for as long as 27 days and as short as 10 days each year. The shifting of the

Earth's energy grids affects the portal's energy. This year's energy grids allow the portal's energy to exist from October 3rd to the 21st.

The bear represents strength, power, authority, while Dubhe has the energy of wisdom, change, and psychic awareness, creating a portal of energy to support strength and decisiveness in decision making. The Bear Gate is strong this year, combining with energy grids currently on the planet. This portal affects the sacral chakra. You may experience others coming into power and dominance as a result.

If you experience indecision or need to make clear decisions, use meditation, cardio exercise, or group retreats to allow the energy to be supported and flow during this time period.

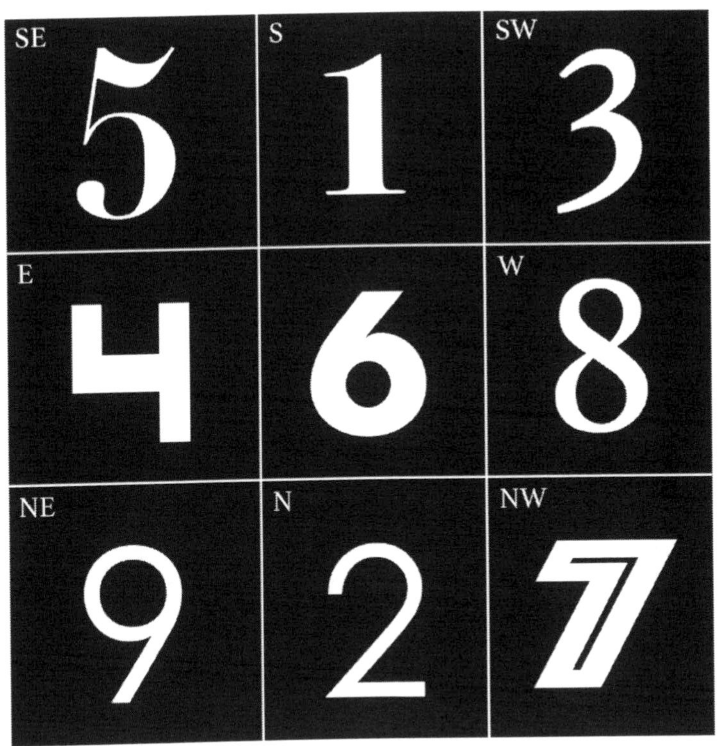

THE FLYING STARS

YEAR OF THE METAL OX

YEAR OF THE METAL OX

February 12, 2021 to January 31, 2022

Feng shui, also known as Chinese geomancy, originates from ancient China, using energy forces to harmonize individuals with their surrounding environment. The word **feng**, meaning wind, and **shui**, meaning water, is the concept of the flow of energy through a space. The Flying Stars add in the influence of the stars' movement affecting the energy of the room. Every year the alignments of the stars change, changing the feng shui energy map. The flying Stars feng shui also considers the person's energy using the birth year in the equation. The feng shui map is divided into 9 sections, using the directional map of North, East, West, and South.

SE	S	SW
5	1	3
E 4	6	W 8
NE 9	N 2	NW 7

You can use this map for your home or office. Use a compass for accuracy. It will better determine your points and sections. Overlay the flying star map to view the association of your 9 areas with the correct star. There are negative and positive influences on the flying stars. For 2021 the positive influence areas are 1, 4, 6, and 8. The area that may be negative or positive this year is 9. The negative influence areas are 2, 3, 5, and 7. Just as in any planetary energy; there is a remedy to effect change just by adding or deleting something within the space. It is always better to remedy negative energy before amplifying positive energy.

Positive Areas for 2021

South: 1 Flying Star, Success

The 1 Star represents intelligence, career, success, fame, and wealth. This star is significantly amplified by people born under the Rat and Tiger signs. A strong year to bring unexpected benefits in personal development for those who use this area for an office, bedroom, living room, or main door entrance.

Energies used to amplify this area:

- Reduce water elements like fish tanks or fountains
- Wood elements
- Green color or plants

East: 4 Flying Star, Love

The 4 Star, Love, relationships, creativity, talent, and luck. This star is amplified by those born under the Goat and Monkey. It also is amplified by mothers of the family. A strong year to bring in the luck of love, marriage proposal, and success in sentimental areas.

Energies used to amplify this area:

- Amethyst or quartz crystals
- Fertility statues
- Dragons for harmony
- Dragonflies for connections
- Reduce woods and bring in metals
- Color red

Center: 6 Flying Star, Luck

The 6 Star, luck, authority, power, wealth, and career. The star is amplified for those born under the Dragon or Snake signs and daughters of the family. A strong year for financial luck, a better life, divine protection, and creative ideas.

Energies used to amplify this area:

- Any symbols of abundance
- Earth elements
- Amber crystals
- Golden colors

West: 8 Flying Star, Wealth and Prosperity

The 8 star represents wealth, health, prosperity, fame, and success. This star is significantly amplified and beneficial for those born under the Dog and Pig's Chinese zodiac signs. Also strong for the head of households and business leaders. A great year to bring in financial prosperity, emotional perseverance, generosity, diligence, vitality, and authority.

Energies used to amplify this area:

- 8 Chinese coins
- Tree of Wealth (Chinese coin tree)
- Ceramics and planters of soil and Earth elements
- Fresh floral plants

Northeast: 9, Flying Star, Future Wealth

The 9 Star, fame, celebration, wealth, intelligence, popularity, prosperity. The star is amplified for those born under the Rooster sign. If the area is a bedroom, office, or living room, the energy is amplified. If the area is a kitchen or entryway, the energy is negative and needs to be strengthened. A strong year for fame, connections, and synchronicity in the positive. Impulsiveness, temptations, and infidelity in the negative making communication important.

Energies to balance the area:

- Jade stones and figurines
- Money jar
- Less traffic through the area
- Less use of metals in the area

Negative areas in 2021

North: 2 Flying Star, Illness

The 2 Star, illness, depression, problems with socialization. This star is amplified by those born under the sign of the Horse. A strong year for sickness for those with the bedroom, main door, or office on the north side of a building. Digestive issues, weight gain, stress, water-related diseases such as kidney and urinary functions.

Energy to balance this area:

- Adding of metal art or figurines brass being the best
- Reduce water features
- Earth colors
- No Construction

Southwest: 3 Flying Star, Disputes

The 3 Star, disputes, legal issues, gossip, conflicting energies. This star amplifies the energies for those born under the sign of the Rat. A strong year for salary and career issues, legal problems, unnecessary expenses, professional training. Avoid stubbornness, excessive pride, aggression. Take care of communications issues right away between loved ones, co-workers, and clients.

Energy to balance this area:

- Candles of any color
- Selenium crystals, or onyx stones
- Green plants
- Remove clutter of any kind

Southeast: 5 Flying Star, Bad luck

The 5 Star, misfortune, illness, accidents, money loss. The star is amplified by those that are born under the Rabbit sign. A strong year for illness and unjustified spending. It could, however, bring in wealth and fame if the energy is balanced in this area.

Energies to balance the area:

- Color red or purple
- Citrines and Aventurine crystals
- Floral scents
- Pink lotus flower in crystal or artwork
- Books and knowledge
- Fire elements

Northwest: 7 Flying Star, Theft

The 7 Star, fighting, arguments, gossip, missing items, money loss. This star amplifies the energy for everyone, therefore all must take precautions. This is a year of greed and temptation, not the best year to borrow money.

Energies to balance the area:

- This is a metal sign; there is a need to reduce all metals in the area to stop it from amplifying
- Add water features, fish tanks, or fountains
- Sodalite, aquamarine, black obsidian, green tourmaline crystals
- Colors of black or blue

THE MASTER CALENDAR

JANUARY

MASTER CALENDAR 2021

FULL MOON		WANING CRESCENT MOON		EQUINOX OR SOLSTICE	
SUPER MOON		RETROGRADE		STAR GATE	
NEW MOON		DORMANT RETROGRADE		ECLIPSE	

SUNDAY	MONDAY	TUESDAY	WEDNESDAY	THURSDAY	FRIDAY	SATURDAY
27	28	29	30	31	1	2
3	4	5	6	7 WANING CRESCENT STARTS	8	9
10	11	12 WANING CRESCENT ENDS	13	14 URANUS STARTS	15	16
17	18	19	20	21	22	23
24	25	26	27	28	29	30 MERCURY STARTS
31	1	2	3	4	5	6

FEBRUARY

MASTER CALENDAR 2021

FULL MOON
SUPER MOON
NEW MOON
WANING CRESCENT MOON
RETROGRADE
DORMANT RETROGRADE
EQUINOX OR SOLSTICE
STAR GATE
ECLIPSE

SUNDAY	MONDAY	TUESDAY	WEDNESDAY	THURSDAY	FRIDAY	SATURDAY
31	1	2	3	4	5 WANING CRESCENT STARTS	6 DEER GATE STARTS
7 MERCURY DORMANT STARTS	8	9	10 WANING CRESCENT ENDS	11 MERCURY DORMANT ENDS	12	13
14 DEER GATE ENDS	15	16	17	18	19 URANUS DORMANT STARTS	20
21 MERCURY ENDS	22	23	24	25	26	27
28	1	2	3	4	5	6

MARCH

MASTER CALENDAR 2021

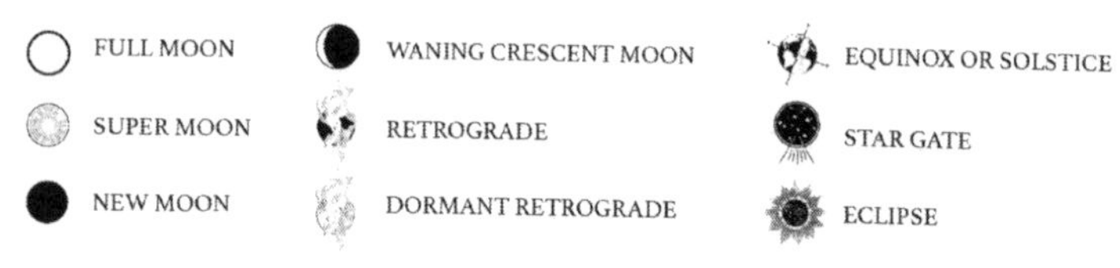

SUNDAY	MONDAY	TUESDAY	WEDNESDAY	THURSDAY	FRIDAY	SATURDAY
28	1	2	3	4	5	6
7 WANING CRESCENT STARTS URANUS DORMANT ENDS	8	9	10	11	12 WANING CRESCENT ENDS	13
14	15	16	17	18	19	20
21	22	23	24	25	26	27
28	29	30	31	1	2	3

APRIL

MASTER CALENDAR 2021

FULL MOON
SUPER MOON
NEW MOON
WANING CRESCENT MOON
RETROGRADE
DORMANT RETROGRADE
EQUINOX OR SOLSTICE
STAR GATE
ECLIPSE

SUNDAY	MONDAY	TUESDAY	WEDNESDAY	THURSDAY	FRIDAY	SATURDAY
28	29	30	31	1	2	3
4	5 WANING CRESCENT STARTS	6	7	8	9	10
11 WANING CRESCENT ENDS	12	13	14	15	16	17
18	19	20	21	22	23	24
25	26	27 PLUTO STARTS	28	29	30	1

MAY

MASTER CALENDAR 2021

FULL MOON
SUPER MOON
NEW MOON
WANING CRESCENT MOON
RETROGRADE
DORMANT RETROGRADE
EQUINOX OR SOLSTICE
STAR GATE
ECLIPSE

SUNDAY	MONDAY	TUESDAY	WEDNESDAY	THURSDAY	FRIDAY	SATURDAY
25	26	27	28	29	30	1
2	3	4 WANING CRESCENT STARTS	5	6	7	8
9	10 WANING CRESCENT ENDS	11	12	13	14	15
16	17	18	19	20	21	22
23 SATURN STARTS	24	25	26 LUNAR	27 PLUTO DORMANT STARTS	28	29
30 MERCURY STARTS	31	1	2	3	4	5

JUNE

MASTER CALENDAR 2021

FULL MOON — WANING CRESCENT MOON — EQUINOX OR SOLSTICE

SUPER MOON — RETROGRADE — STAR GATE

NEW MOON — DORMANT RETROGRADE — ECLIPSE

SUNDAY	MONDAY	TUESDAY	WEDNESDAY	THURSDAY	FRIDAY	SATURDAY
30	31	1	2	3 WANING CRESCENT STARTS	4	5
6	7	8 MERCURY DORMANT STARTS	9 WANING CRESCENT ENDS	10	11	12 MERCURY DORMANT ENDS
13	14	15	16	17	18	19
20 PLUTO DORMANT ENDS; JUPITER STARTS	21	22	23 MERCURY ENDS	24	25 NEPTUNE STARTS	26
27	28	29	30	1	2	3
4	5	6	7	8	9	10

JULY

MASTER CALENDAR 2021

FULL MOON
SUPER MOON
NEW MOON
WANING CRESCENT MOON
RETROGRADE
DORMANT RETROGRADE
EQUINOX OR SOLSTICE
STAR GATE
ECLIPSE

SUNDAY	MONDAY	TUESDAY	WEDNESDAY	THURSDAY	FRIDAY	SATURDAY
27	28	29	30	1	2 WANING CRESCENT STARTS	3
4	5	6	7	8 JUPITER DORMANT STARTS	9 WANING CRESCENT ENDS	10 SOLAR
11	12	13	14 SATURN DORMANT STARTS	15 JUPITER DORMANT ENDS	16	17
18	19	20	21	22	23	24
25	26	27	28	29	30	31
1	2	3	4	5	6	7

AUGUST

MASTER CALENDAR 2021

FULL MOON	WANING CRESCENT MOON	EQUINOX OR SOLSTICE
SUPER MOON	RETROGRADE	STAR GATE
NEW MOON	DORMANT RETROGRADE	ECLIPSE

SUNDAY	MONDAY	TUESDAY	WEDNESDAY	THURSDAY	FRIDAY	SATURDAY
1 WANING CRESCENT STARTS	2	3	4	5 LION'S GATE STARTS; SATURN DORMANT ENDS	6	7 WANING CRESCENT ENDS
8	9	10 LION'S GATE ENDS	11	12	13	14
15	16	17	18	19	20 URANUS ENDS	21
22	23	24	25	26 NEPTUNE DORMANT STARTS	27	28
29	30	31	1	2	3	4
5	6	7	8	9	10	11

SEPTEMBER

MASTER CALENDAR 2021

FULL MOON	WANING CRESCENT MOON	EQUINOX OR SOLSTICE
SUPER MOON	RETROGRADE	STAR GATE
NEW MOON	DORMANT RETROGRADE	ECLIPSE

SUNDAY	MONDAY	TUESDAY	WEDNESDAY	THURSDAY	FRIDAY	SATURDAY
29	30	31	1 WANING CRESCENT STARTS	2	3	4
5	6 WANING CRESCENT ENDS	7	8	9	10	11
12	13	14 NEPTUNE DORMANT ENDS	15	16	17	18
19	20	21	22	23	24	25
26	27 MERCURY STARTS	28	29	30 WANING CRESCENT STARTS	1	2
3	4	5	6	7	8	9

OCTOBER

MASTER CALENDAR 2021

FULL MOON
SUPER MOON
NEW MOON
WANING CRESCENT MOON
RETROGRADE
DORMANT RETROGRADE
EQUINOX OR SOLSTICE
STAR GATE
ECLIPSE

SUNDAY	MONDAY	TUESDAY	WEDNESDAY	THURSDAY	FRIDAY	SATURDAY
26	27	28	29	30	1	2
3 BEAR GATE STARTS	4 MERCURY DORMANT STARTS	5 WANING CRESCENT ENDS	6 PLUTO ENDS	7	8 MERCURY DORMANT ENDS	9
10	11 SATURN ENDS	12	13	14	15	16
17 JUPITER ENDS	18 MERCURY ENDS	19	20	21 BEAR GATE ENDS	22	23
24	25	26	27	28	29 WANING CRESCENT STARTS	30
31	1	2	3	4	5	6

NOVEMBER

MASTER CALENDAR 2021

FULL MOON
WANING CRESCENT MOON
EQUINOX OR SOLSTICE
SUPER MOON
RETROGRADE
STAR GATE
NEW MOON
DORMANT RETROGRADE
ECLIPSE

SUNDAY	MONDAY	TUESDAY	WEDNESDAY	THURSDAY	FRIDAY	SATURDAY
31	1	2	3 WANING CRESCENT ENDS	4	5	6
7	8	9	10	11	12	13
14	15	16	17	18	19 LUNAR	20
21	22	23	24	25	26	27
28 WANING CRESCENT STARTS	29	30	1	2	3	4
5	6	7	8	9	10	11

DECEMBER

MASTER CALENDAR 2021

FULL MOON
SUPER MOON
NEW MOON
WANING CRESCENT MOON
RETROGRADE
DORMANT RETROGRADE
EQUINOX OR SOLSTICE
STAR GATE
ECLIPSE

SUNDAY	MONDAY	TUESDAY	WEDNESDAY	THURSDAY	FRIDAY	SATURDAY
28	29	30	1 NEPTUNE ENDS	2	3 WANING CRESCENT ENDS	4 SOLAR
5	6	7	8	9	10	11
12	13	14	15	16	17	18
19 VENUS STARTS	20	21	22	23	24	25
26	27	28 WANING CRESCENT STARTS VENUS DORMANT STARTS	29	30	31	1
2	3	4	5	6	7	8

GLOSSARY OF TERMINOLOGY

Alignment: In spiritual terms, meaning the flow of energy, to be able to receive and give.

Autumnal Equinox: The position of the sun crossing the equator in the Autumn, day and night are of equal length.

Chakra: The 12 major energy centers for the body that transfer energy from the body to the environment or spiritual plane and vice versa.

Eclipse: The light of the moon blocked by the position of the Earth between it and the sun (lunar eclipse) or the light of the sun blocked by the position of the moon between it and a point on the Earth (solar eclipse).

Energy Grid: An interconnected map containing a spectrum of energies.

Equinox: The time when the sun crosses the Earth's equator, making night and day equal in length all over the Earth. Occurs twice a year, about March 20 (vernal equinox, or spring equinox) and September 22 (autumnal equinox).

Feng Shui: Also known as Chinese geomancy, is a pseudoscientific traditional practice originating from ancient China, which claims to use energy forces to harmonize individuals with their surrounding environment.

Flying Stars Feng Shui: The integration of the principles of Yin Yang, the interactions between the five elements, the eight trigrams, the Lo Shu numbers, and the 24 Mountains, by using time, space and objects to create an astrological chart to analyze positive and negative energies of a building.

Full Moon: The last lunar phase when the moon is a whole disk is illuminated, occurring when in opposition to the sun.

New Moon: The first lunar phase, when the Moon and Sun have the same ecliptic longitude.

Palo Santo: Is a wild tree native from the Yucatan Peninsula to Peru and Venezuela. The tree belongs to the same family as frankincense and myrrh. The most popular use of Palo Santo is the ritual purification by burning of the wood.

Portal: A transportation vehicle for energy with connections from one place to another, allowing the alignment of the flow of energy.

Retrograde: Moving backward; having a backward motion or direction; retiring or retreating. An optical illusion of the planets traveling around the sun.

Sage Burning: Purification ritual of burning the sage to cleanse the energy within a space.

Sea Salt Cleansing Bath: Soaking bath consistent with the salt levels of the sea to cleanse the negative energy from the spiritual and physical bodies.

Shuman Resonance: A set of spectrum peaks in the extremely low frequency (ELF) portion of the Earth's electromagnetic field spectrum.

Solstice: Either of the two times in the year, the summer solstice and the winter solstice, when the sun reaches its highest or lowest point in the sky at noon, marked by the longest and shortest days.

Star Gate: A portal within the universe that allows rapid travel of energy between two distant locations.

Super Moon: The moon appears particularly large in the sky due to the coincidence of its closest approach to the Earth with a full moon.

Vortex: A strong electromagnetic mass of energy that is constantly in flux, maybe a positive or a negative energy force due to combining several energy grids together.

Wanning Crescent Moon: The moon appears to be partly, but less than half illuminated by direct sunlight. This Moon can be seen after the last quarter moon and right before the new Moon.

Waxing Crescent Moon: The Moon becomes visible again after the New Moon conjunction, when the Sun and Earth were on opposite sides of the Moon, the crescent refers to the curved shape similar to a banana or a boat.

SHERRY HOPSON

Sherry Hopson is an internationally known author, speaker and radio personality. Her Corporate background includes 30 years of experience in Management, Consulting (Human Resources and Business development), and Finance. She has also held a position of CSO (Chief Spiritual Office) on the Board of Directors for an Import/Export Company. She left the corporate world to follow her passion as a spiritual counselor.

She specializes in the technique of transformational therapy, utilizing her skills as a psychic and a healer. The foundation of her practice is the how, what, why and where of energy that creates karma and forms emotional intelligence. After identifying disruptive energy patterns, she uses a process of clearing, transforming & analyzing belief systems to align to desired outcomes for her clients.

Learn more at www.SherryHopson.com

WALLIS SUDA

Wallis Suda is an Art Director working across Fashion, Interiors, and Wellness. Disciplined at Parsons School of Design in NY and Paris, her philosophy of design is built on a foundation that the right balance of academic knowledge in global design, art, raw materials, current affairs and interactions with all types of people is the formula to creating radical product inspiring emotion, dialogue and healing. She has worked for international brands such as Calvin Klein.

Wallis' greatest skill is to take the dreams of others as well as her own and bring them into physical reality. She believes in building experiences through the design and curation of beautiful objects, art, textiles, food, music, people, horticulture and spirituality in a manner that is unique to each project. The idea is not to create more, but to create beauty out of what exists for a new golden age.

Learn more at www.WallisSuda.com